THE ROLE AND CONTROL OF
WEAPONS IN THE 1990s

THE OPERATIONAL LEVEL OF WAR
Edited by Michael Krause, Deputy Chief of the US Army Center for Military History, and Andrew Wheatcroft

The Operational Level of War series provides for a theory of armed conflicts in the present and the immediate future. Unlike many theories, it is not rooted in abstractions but in the practice of war, both in history and the immediate past.

The books in the series all contribute to the clearer understanding of the potentials and the dangers of war in the 1990s.

The key contribution of the operational theory of war is to provide a link between strategy and tactics, a connection which is of unique importance in modern warfare.

THE ROLE AND CONTROL OF WEAPONS IN THE 1990s

Frank Barnaby

R Routledge

London and New York

First published 1992
by Routledge
11 New Fetter Lane, London EC4P 4EE

Simultaneously published in the USA and Canada
by Routledge
a division of Routledge, Chapman and Hall, Inc.
29 West 35th Street, New York, NY 10001

© 1992 Frank Barnaby

Typeset in 10/12pt Palatino by
Intype, London
Printed in Great Britain by
T J Press (Padstow) Ltd, Padstow, Cornwall

British Library Cataloguing in Publication Data
Barnaby, Frank
Role and Control of Weapons in the 1990s
I. Title
355

Library of Congress Cataloging-in-Publication Data

Barnaby, Frank.
The role and control of weapons in the 1990's / Frank Barnaby.
p. cm.
Includes bibliographical references and index.
1. Military readiness. 2. Europe—Defenses. 3. Arms control.
I. Title.
UA10.B37   1992
355'.033'0049—dc20   92-9373

ISBN 0-415-07673-0

CONTENTS

LIST OF TABLES

INTRODUCTION

The revolutions which ended communist rule in eastern Europe and the Soviet Union at the end of the 1980s were peaceful processes. The establishment of new orders in these countries during the 1990s will almost certainly be a much more violent process.

The transformation of the Soviet Union – a one-party state with a failed economic system – to the Commonwealth of Independent States – a collection of independent, politically pluralist republics run as market economies – is the most ambitious political task undertaken in the past hundred years. But the move from communism to democracy is unlikely to be carried through peacefully everywhere.

Moves to democracy are a reason for optimism because history shows that democratic states are the least likely to go to war against each other. It is, therefore, encouraging that democracy and the rule of law are also spreading in the Third World.

Some European neighbours may feel threatened by events in the former Soviet Union. But the military threat to western Europe has essentially disappeared with the reunification of Germany, the collapse of the Warsaw Pact and the disintegration of the Soviet Union.

Old threats to European security have disappeared, but new ones are emerging. They arise from: nationalism, resulting in numerous nationalist tensions in Europe and the former Soviet Union; the risk of the escalation of war in other regions, including the Middle East, and the Indian sub-continent; the spread of chemical, biological and nuclear weapons and missile technology to unstable regions; and global problems, such as environmental degradation, world population increase, the debt crisis, and the poverty gap and north–south tension.

The solution of global problems will require the investment of considerable amounts of money and, more important, the skills of many scientists and engineers. These financial and manpower resources can be most easily taken from the military. Many hope, therefore, that some of the current reductions in the resources given to the military will be diverted to assist, and make sustainable, the development of Third World countries.

During the Cold War enormous sums of money were given to the military–industrial complex. In the 1950s, for example, annual world military expenditure was typically thirty times more, in real terms (to take inflation into account), than annual world military expenditure in the decade before the Second World War. During the last twenty-five years of the Cold War, 1965–90, world military spending increased, in real terms (1990 prices), from about $560,000 million to about $950,000 million.

Military budgets are now falling, although at a rather modest rate. A real reduction in world military spending of about 5 per cent a year can be reasonably expected for the next few years.

But spending on military research and development is not decreasing. Nor is it likely to do so in the foreseeable future. In fact, it may well increase. So far as Third World development is concerned, this is most depressing.

Currently, the funds given to military science amount to about $100,000 million a year. More than 500,000 research scientists and engineers (about 20 per cent of the world's research scientists and engineers) are engaged full-time in developing weapons. Unless a large fraction of these professionals is diverted to the solution of Third World problems, it is very hard to see how these problems can be solved.

The fast-changing face of Europe raises many security issues, regional and global, and requires new security arrangements. Is east–west _détente_ here to stay? Will new enemy images be formed? Now that the Americans have achieved their historical goal – of being the only global superpower – how will they use their power?

How will European defence be organized in the future? What structures are appropriate for European defence? Will America be prepared to stay in Europe under European leadership or must it dominate?

What relations should evolve between the various European institutions – NATO, the Western European Union, the Conference on Co-operation and Security in Europe, and so on? Can a pan-European defence be evolved?

New military technologies are giving the military unprecedented capabilities. What options do they offer for military postures? Is non-offensive defence the optimum military policy for many countries?

If there is to be a new world order, there must, it is generally assumed, be some control of the arms trade. How large is the global arms trade? What are the prospects for controlling it? Why do countries buy and sell weapons?

A major threat to global security is the proliferation of ballistic missiles to Third World countries. This threat will be considerably enhanced if ballistic missiles fitted with nuclear, chemical or biological warheads spread. Can effective regimes be established to control the spread of ballistic missiles and of weapons of mass destruction?

How seriously should we take the risk that sub-national groups, including terrorists, will acquire weapons of mass destruction? How easy is it to make a nuclear explosive? Could terrorists effectively make and disperse chemical nerve agents or biological agents?

Arms-control and disarmament treaties normally take so long to negotiate that the process does not suit the conditions in the post-Cold War world. Unilateral reductions may become the preferred method of disarmament. The stage may have been set by the unilateral initiatives of Presidents Bush and Gorbachev to reduce considerably American and Soviet nuclear arsenals. But verification of arms reductions, however, achieved, will remain crucial. What technologies are available for verification?

For the first time since the nuclear age began, far-reaching nuclear disarmament is on the cards. But current proposals will not stop the nuclear arms race. The drive for a nuclear strategic superiority will go on – particularly, it seems, in the USA. A comprehensive ban on all nuclear-weapon tests remains, therefore, an urgently needed arms-control measure.

Equally urgent is the need to control the damage done in modern war. Recent wars have brought home dramatically the great destructiveness of modern weapons, including new powerful conventional warheads. There is an obvious need to control both the human costs and the environmental impacts of modern war. How could this be best achieved? By banning specific weapons or by a comprehensive and unambiguous convention prohibiting the use of environmental damage as a weapon of war?

1

THE EVOLUTION OF SECURITY

Before the First World War, national security, and the role of military forces, was concerned almost entirely with the protection of the nation's territory from invasion and occupation, and, for those countries which had them, with the policing of colonies. After the 1917 Bolshevik revolution, many non-communist states became concerned about subversion, both internal and external, and security was broadened to include the protection of the state's political and social values – values usually defined by the establishment in each country. After the Second World War, a third element was added to national security: the need to protect the nation's strategic markets and sources of raw materials.

Recent changes in the international situation, particularly the end of the Cold War, are focusing attention on the need to redefine national security to take into account growing threats arising from a variety of global problems. For example, the rapidly increasing world population and the widening gap between the rich and poor countries is increasing north–south tension to such an extent that it may soon be greater than east–west tension ever was.

The consequences of north–south tension are beginning to affect the security debate in countries in the northern hemisphere. And increasing pressures on non-renewable resources – water, fertile land, fish, and so on – are increasingly recognized as major sources of conflict between Third World countries. There is, therefore, a growing awareness that the need to ameliorate the impact of global problems is a new element of national security.

The security of all regions has been considerably complicated by the end of the Cold War. But the greatest impact has been on European security.

European security

In many ways, European security issues were simpler during the Cold War, when both sides obeyed the rules of the game – NATO countries did not interfere in eastern European affairs, and the Warsaw Pact kept out of NATO's affairs. By and large, the collective security of the military alliances maintained a certain stability (although not real peace). The problem was that all Europeans were living with the fear of a nuclear holocaust.

Now that the Cold War is over, and that the Warsaw Pact is no longer in existence, the threat of nuclear war in Europe has been largely removed. Only the most reactionary people now believe that the former Soviet Union (now the Commonwealth of Independent States) is a significant military threat to western Europe. But other threats to European security have emerged.

The communist regimes in eastern Europe and the Soviet Union kept the lid on nationalism in these countries. Now that these regimes have collapsed, and the Soviet Union has disintegrated into independent republics, nationalism has reappeared as a major source of conflict in Europe. European security problems of the 1990s may well be similar to those of Europe before the world wars.

Instabilities in eastern Europe most obviously relate to domestic conflicts within the former communist states in eastern Europe and a disintegrating Soviet Union. But some of the bilateral disputes between the countries will almost certainly flare up into armed conflict during the 1990s. The list of bilateral disputes in eastern Europe is a long one, bringing home the extent of instability in the region.

Nelson, for example, lists the following bilateral disputes: the dispute between Greece and Yugoslavia about Macedonia and the future of Greece's northern border; tensions between Greece and Albania caused by some 350,000 ethnic Greeks in Albania and the Albanian minority in northern Greece; tensions between Romania and the Moldavian Republic caused by the desire of the ethnic Romanian majority for independence and demands for a unified Romanian–Moldavian state; the dispute between Bulgaria and Turkey about the very large Turkish minority in north-eastern and south-western Bulgaria; friction between Bulgaria and Romania caused by, for example, the Bulgarian minority living in the Romanian portion of Dobrudja; tensions between Poland and Germany caused by, among other factors, the ownership of property in Poland once owned by Germans, navigation rights in the Baltic, and the German minority living in Poland; tensions provoked by Polish nationalists in Belorussia, the Ukraine and Lithuania – well over a million ethnic Poles are scattered through the territory of the disintegrating Soviet Union; tensions between Hungary and

2

Romania caused by Hungarian claims that the large number of ethnic Hungarians in Romanian Transylvania are being denied economic or political rights; tensions between Albania and Yugoslavia over the ethnic Albanians who make up 90 per cent of the population of Kosovo, a province of Serbia; the dispute between Bulgaria and Yugoslavia over Macedonia; and the dispute between Greece and Turkey over the Aegean (Nelson, Spring 1991). Long though this list is, it is by no means exhaustive.

Apart from the threats to European security originating within the region, there is a risk that a war in some unstable region outside Europe will spread to Europe. Now that Soviet and American competition for client states in the Third World has largely ended this risk has considerably diminished but has not disappeared. The threats to Europe that are growing are those emerging from global problems – such as those related to increasing Third World populations, poverty and pollution.

The changing spectrum of threats to the security of European countries is, not very surprisingly, provoking much discussion about the future of NATO. By 1994, all military forces of the former Soviet Union should be out of eastern Europe. Even if disaffection in the former Soviet Union leads to a takeover by the military or the KGB the military threat to Europe is hardly likely to be serious. NATO was formed in response to the perception of a Soviet military threat. Now that the Warsaw Pact has collapsed, Germany is reunified and the military threat of the former Soviet Union to western Europe has virtually disappeared, what strategy and military force structure should NATO adopt?

At their summit meeting in Rome in November 1991, NATO's political leaders endorsed the Alliance's new post-Cold War strategy. In spite of high-sounding words, NATO's so-called 'new strategic concept' turns out to be a damp squib; it is little more than a rehash of the old policy.

The profound changes that have taken place in eastern Europe and the former Soviet Union have transformed the security environment in which NATO operates. It is, therefore, truly remarkable that the sixteen leaders of the Alliance found it impossible to agree on more significant changes. NATO seems unable to face the fact that the Cold War is over, the Warsaw Pact no longer exists and a disintegrating Soviet Union is no military threat to anyone.

But NATO stubbornly refuses to change its policy of threatening to be the first to use nuclear weapons in a conventional war – an absurd hangover from the Cold War. In spite of this, the number of nuclear weapons deployed in Europe is being reduced from about 3,500 to about 700.

3

A fly on the wall at the Rome meeting would have concluded that all is sweetness and light in NATO. There was, for example, agreement that there should be 'a more institutional relationship of consultation and cooperation on political and security issues' with the Soviet Union, the Baltic Republics and the eastern European countries.

But the eastern European members of the former Warsaw Pact will not be allowed to join NATO; Czechoslovakia's recent application for some sort of association with NATO was firmly rejected. And eastern European countries will not even be included in NATO's guarantee against aggression. The decision to keep others out – a bitter disappointment to many of the eastern European countries – is another sign that NATO still clings doggedly to Cold War thinking.

There is serious disagreement about how NATO's military strategy should evolve. Basically, the disagreement is between those, particularly Britain supported to some extent by Italy, who want no dilution of NATO's role in western Europe's defence and those, particularly France and Germany, who want a purely European security identity and a separate European army.

Those, like the British, who want to maintain NATO in its present form at all costs do so because they do not want to weaken the Atlantic alliance; they want to keep the Americans directly involved in European defence for the foreseeable future. The others believe that European and American interests will diverge significantly over the coming years and believe that the USA will withdraw eventually from European defence.

The basic disagreement is, then, over the future role of the USA in European defence. The British believe that there should be a continuing American role in European defence and they want NATO to survive intact to make sure that it continues. France, on the other hand, wants to make the European Community entirely responsible for Europe's defence.

Not very surprisingly, the Americans do not want to lose their position as top dog in NATO. But American dominance will, to say the least, be hard to justify in a politically united Europe. Hence the French, and German, pressure for change.

The French believe that a resurrected Western European Union rather than NATO should be responsible for Europe's military forces. It makes little sense, it argues, for the European Community to unite economically and politically unless it develops common defence and foreign policies.

Although Britain agrees that the European defence identity should be strengthened, and that the WEU should be involved in it, she wants NATO decisions as well as European Community ones to guide the WEU. The British want no separate role for the WEU within the

4

NATO area. But they have no objection to the WEU being responsible for any military action taken by western European forces outside the NATO area.

Although the details of NATO's new strategy are still obscure, its military forces are, nevertheless, being radically restructured. NATO's forces will consist of four types. The first type will be an Immediate Reaction Force, equipped to react to a crisis virtually immediately, or at least at very short notice. This brigade-sized, highly mobile force will ideally be made up of small numbers of troops from as many NATO nations as possible, to show solidarity. The idea is that the Immediate Reaction Force could be deployed without lengthy political discussions.

The second type of NATO force will be a new Rapid Reaction Force, consisting of about 70,000 troops. It will be equipped to deploy rapidly to any area of crisis within NATO Europe – from northern Norway to eastern Turkey. The military commander of the Rapid Reaction Force will be a British lieutenant-general, and British forces will provide two of its four divisions, one of them based in the UK. A third division will be a multinational air mobile division. The composition of the fourth division has not yet been announced. The Rapid Reaction Force will include about one-sixth of NATO's total forces.

If it is decided that European national interests require the use of military forces in places where, for political reasons, NATO cannot itself act, the Rapid Reaction Force may operate under the auspices of the WEU.

The third type of NATO forces will be the Main Defence Forces, kept in a lower state of readiness than the Rapid Reaction Force. They will provide the bulk of NATO defence. Mainly deployed in Germany, this multinational force will include, for example, the German Bundeswehr and the American Army Corps that is to remain in Germany. Only German troops will be stationed in the eastern part of Germany until the troops of the former Soviet Union leave.

The fourth type of NATO forces will be the so-called Augmentation Force, consisting mainly of reserves and kept in a low state of readiness, to be mobilized over a period of weeks or even months.

Plans to restructure NATO forces are complicated by the fact that all NATO countries are reducing their national forces and reviewing their contribution to NATO. According to current plans, the strength of the British army, for example, is being reduced from about 150,000 troops to about 100,000 and will possibly eventually be reduced to about 80,000.

Big reductions, typically of between 25 and 30 per cent, will also be made in the forces of the other European allies. And the Americans plan to halve their land and air forces in Germany, to about 150,000 troops, as the troops of the former Soviet Union are withdrawn from eastern Europe. The American troop reduction should be completed by the mid-1990s.

As eastern European countries and the newly independent Soviet republics become more economically and politically associated with western Europe, it is likely that the 38-nation Conference on Co-operation and Security in Europe (CSCE) process will, in the longer term, evolve a pan-European defence role. Some NATO leaders recognize that, in the meantime, the CSCE should be given a peace-keeping role throughout Europe.

Many fundamental questions about the future of NATO, and of European defence, remain unanswered. To what extent should NATO co-operate with yesterday's enemies – the eastern European countries and the Commonwealth of Independent States? How will the eastern European security vacuum be filled? How should such co-operation be arranged? Should American troops remain in Europe? What role should British and French nuclear weapons be given? What mechanisms should be evolved for crisis management and peace-keeping in Europe? How will the various European institutions – the WEU, NATO, the CSCE and the European Community – relate to each other? Is serious thought being given to mechanisms for an eventual pan-European defence?

Until NATO shakes off its Cold War thinking, it will be unable to grapple effectively with these issues. Unfortunately, it looks as though this will take some time.

Responding to changing patterns of violence in the 1990s

The role of military force, in general, will almost certainly change drastically during the next decade. The military forces of the developed countries will, for example, probably be increasingly involved in controlling terrorism and the international drugs trade, in disaster relief, and in evacuating nationals from foreign countries at war. These military activities will help make future military budgets publicly acceptable.

Total military budgets – at least, in most European and other developed countries – will almost certainly decrease significantly over the next few years. But more resources will probably be devoted to military research and development, reflecting the continuing effort to achieve and maintain military technological superiority. Not only are there powerful vested interests – academic and industrial intent on increasing these budgets, but also some countries – the USA and Israel are typical examples – set great store by keeping abreast of all advances in military technology. To be ahead in military science is believed to be an essential element of national security.)

Funds given to military research and development (R & D) are currently running worldwide at a total of about $100,000 million a year. But to continue investing such large resources in military science in today's world is immoral and unwise. Immoral because the research talent now monopolized by military science is needed to tackle urgent global problems; and unwise because advances in military technology, if allowed to continue unabated, will lead, *détente* notwithstanding, to perceptions of a nuclear first-strike capability which will destabilize international relations and considerably increase the risk of nuclear war, particularly accidental or unintentional nuclear war.

About 60 million people – roughly equivalent to the entire labour force in European manufacturing industries – are absorbed in military or military-related activities. Many of them are highly qualified. The most qualified are those working in military R & D.

The world's research scientists and engineers total about 2.5 million. Of these, about 500,000 (20 per cent) work only on military R & D. If only physicists and engineering scientists are included, the percentage is even greater. Over 50 per cent of the world's research physicists and engineering scientists are military scientists. Put another way, military science absorbs scientific and technological capabilities ten times greater than those available to *all* the developing countries.

Although more resources will be devoted to military R & D, the control of the spread of offensive conventional weapons and weapons of mass destruction – nuclear, chemical and biological – will increasingly occupy diplomats. Advances in military technology will certainly complicate military policies. New conventional weapons are making the battlefield so lethal that humans will refuse to fight on them. Already, conventional war between industrialized countries would be so destructive as to be unacceptable. Major wars between industrialized countries can, therefore, be virtually discounted.

But the frequency of wars in the Third World is, for the foreseeable future, unlikely to decrease. And the Gulf War is unlikely to be the last war between industrialized and Third World countries. Moreover, as the world population increases, urbanization will increase. Urban guerrilla violence, and with it international terrorism, will increase proportionally.

The world population may, according to demographers, increase from today's 5,300 billion to about 10 billion by 2030. The bulk of this increase will occur in the Third World, and most of the Third World increase will go into cities so that huge metropolises will be formed, with populations of tens, and even hundreds, of millions. Many inhabitants of these huge cities will live in abject poverty in shanty towns with inadequate access to medical services, safe water, food, housing and so on.

These are just the conditions in which urban violence and terrorism grow and flourish. Future terrorists will probably be able to acquire, through the global arms trade, sophisticated weapons, including long-range ballistic missiles equipped with nuclear, chemical or biological warheads. They will also be able to deliver weapons of mass destruction by simpler methods – perhaps carried in ships.

In the next century, problems arising from a huge world population are likely to dominate the security policies of all nations. The finite earth's carrying capacity will probably be unable to cope adequately with the populations, even though technological advances are likely to allow a somewhat higher world population than today's to be supported. If the world population approaches 10 billion or so, disasters – war, pestilence, famine – are inevitable.

The global problems arising from the population explosion (the food crisis, pollution, and the urgent need to develop new sources of energy and raw materials while preserving currently available resources, and poverty (the need to improve health, diet, housing, and education standards) are well known. The skills monopolized by military science are vital for, and could rapidly be diverted to, many of these global problems. If we don't so divert these skills, the rich–poor poverty gap and, therefore, north–south tension will inevitably increase until they become a direct threat to world security.

Conclusions

The shift in emphasis from 'high-intensity conflict' to various types of 'low-intensity conflict' will stimulate changes in military postures and, in the longer term, the evolution of new security systems. In the developed world, security arrangements will take into account global (non-military) threats – such as those from environmental degradation, the north–south poverty gap, pressures on non-renewable resources, and increasing international crime and terrorism.

Be this as it may, during the 1990s the USA will be the dominant global military power. But economic and geopolitical power will increasingly rival military power in determining 'superpower' status, to the advantage of Japan and Germany. The USA may well be prepared to put some of its military forces at the disposal of the United Nations for peace-keeping and conflict management. If so, *Pax United Nations* may replace *Pax Americana*. European countries could greatly assist this process by announcing their willingness to put that (relatively small) part of their military forces earmarked for rapid deployment at the disposal of the United Nations, if asked to do so.

Early in the next century, advances in military technology may result in completely automated warfare. Military vehicles, like armoured vehicles and aircraft, will be driven by robots. If used for aggression, these vehicles will be attacked with automatic missiles. There will be no humans on the battlefield. Will this reduce warfare to absurdity? If not, how will victory be determined? Fundamental changes in the philosophy of war and the use of force are virtually certain.

2

NEW MILITARY TECHNOLOGIES

The systematic destruction in the Gulf War of Iraq by high-technology weapons, and Iraq's inability to respond, was a dramatic demonstration of the overwhelming superiority of the military technology of the industrialized powers. The Gulf War demonstrated the operational effectiveness of a range of new technologies.

New military technologies

For convenience, the most important new military technologies can be grouped under four headings:

1 technologies which provide long-range and real-time surveillance and target acquisition;
2 sensor and guidance technologies for smart and ultra-smart 'fire-and-forget' missiles – able to detect, identify and effectively attack armoured vehicles, combat aircraft and warships, as well as hardened fixed targets like command and control centres, in all weathers and battlefield conditions, and, once fired, without further instructions from the launching platform;
3 very powerful conventional warheads, of improved yield-to-weight ratios; and
4 computerized command, control, communications and intelligence systems.

Reconnaissance

Advances in real-time and long-range surveillance and target-acquisition technologies, for example, have given the military unprecedented reconnaissance capabilities. It is now possible to identify and track, in real time, enemy forces deep in their own territory.

Sensors on board satellites, manned aircraft and remotely piloted vehicles (pilotless aircraft) give advance warning of mobilization and

10

preparations for attack. Rapid advances are being made in a broad range of sensors – photographic and return-beam vidicon television cameras, multi-spectral scanners, visible and infra-red radiometers and microwave synthetic aperture radars, charged couple devices, sensors sensitive to gamma-rays, X-rays and electronic signals, and communications-monitoring devices.

A typical modern surveillance system is the US Joint Surveillance and Target Attack Radar System (JSTARS), an airborne radar system for target acquisition, tracking and weapons-guidance over relatively long ranges. Flying over friendly territory, at some 50 kilometres from the border, the side-looking radar is able to locate tanks and other moving targets at ranges of 150 kilometres or more.

The real-time data collected by JSTARS is passed to a control station for computer analysis. Appropriate weapons, normally missiles, are chosen to attack the targets. The JSTARS radar guides the weapons during their flight to deliver them to their targets with great accuracy. Other JSTARS sensors are able to detect and locate enemy systems that are emitting electromagnetic radiation (radio waves, radar, etc.).

Long-range reconnaissance equipment will be increasingly carried by remotely piloted vehicles (RPVs) rather than by manned aircraft. RPVs are, because of their small size, less vulnerable to air defence systems and, because they are much cheaper than manned aircraft, can be used in relatively large numbers.

Weapon guidance

Modern weapons can be guided to their targets with great accuracy by real-time mid-course guidance and, more important, by terminal guidance. Accuracy is, or soon will be, virtually independent of range. Terminally guided missiles use radar or a laser system to search the area around the target and compare it with a map pre-programmed into the warhead's computer. The system locks on to some fixed location near the target and guides the warhead precisely on to it.

Terminally guided sub-munitions – various varieties of bomblet and mine – are being developed which can distinguish between different types of moving vehicle and attack them at their weakest point (such as the turret of a tank).

Missiles are not only becoming more accurate; they are becoming autonomous. Once fired, an autonomous missile – also called a 'fire-and-forget' missile – seeks out its target, identifies it and attacks it without any further instructions from the person or platform which fired the missile.

New conventional warheads

An example of a new powerful conventional warhead is the fuel–air explosive, used by coalition forces during the 1991 Gulf War. The weapon produces an aerosol cloud of a substance like propylene oxide vapour. When mixed with air, the substance is very explosive; and the aerosol cloud, ignited when at its optimum size, produces a very powerful explosion, between five and ten times as effective, weight for weight, as high explosive.

Several clouds of fuel–air explosive can be formed close together so that when ignited they produce a huge explosion. This can be so large as to be equivalent to that of a low-yield nuclear explosion. People under the exploding cloud die from asphyxiation caused by physical damage to the membranes of their lungs. The fireball produced by the exploding aerosol cloud can kill and injure people on the edge of the explosion.

Cluster bombs and fragmentation munitions are other new conventional weapons. Exploding fragmentation bomblets can scatter small jagged chunks of metal over a large area. The fragments have razor-sharp edges, are very hot, and travel at high speeds. A rocket warhead can carry very large numbers of fragmentation munitions.

Most of the people in the range of the fragments are killed, many of them literally shredded. Those that escape immediate death often have multiple wounds, difficult to treat. Some fragmentation munitions are made of plastic. The fragments in the bodies of survivors do not then show up on X-rays, which greatly complicates medical treatment.

The Vought Multiple-Launch Rocket System (MLRS) fires rockets carrying cluster munitions with anti-personnel bomblets. Each rocket, about 4 metres long and 23 centimetres in diameter, contains 644 bomblets. A salvo of twelve rockets can be fired in about forty-five seconds, and there is a reload time of ten minutes. The range of MLRS is more than 30 kilometres. Each salvo of MLRS rockets, containing nearly 8,000 bomblets, can cover an area of 60 acres or so with anti-personnel fragments, making it as lethal as a low-yield nuclear weapon.

MLRS rockets can also carry shaped-charge anti-tank bomblets. Other warheads being developed for the rockets include a cluster munition with twenty-eight parachute-retarded anti-tank mines, and a cluster munition with six terminally guided (using active radar) free-fall anti-tank shaped-charge bomblets.

Computerized C3I systems

Put simply, a typical military battle takes place in four distinct phases. In the first phase, the enemy forces are located, identified and tracked. The mission is to find out where enemy forces will attack and with what forces. In the second phase, the threat posed by the enemy forces is assessed and decisions are made about how to neutralize it. In the third phase, appropriate weapons to deal with the threat are chosen and fired at the hostile forces. Finally, the damage done to the enemy forces is assessed by reconnaissance to determine whether or not the threat has been removed. If it has not, the sequence is repeated until it has been removed.

The first and last phases of the battle are carried out by military intelligence; the second and third phases are called command and control: orders are exchanged by commanders by military communications systems. The sequence is called command, control, communications and intelligence or C3I.

Military intelligence uses a vast network of sensors for reconnaissance. Command and control uses navigational systems of various types to determine precisely the position of friendly forces and the co-ordinates of targets for weapon systems. So much information is collected by today's reconnaissance and target-acquisition systems that it must be analysed by computer to sort out the information which is useful to commanders from the rest. Military command and control centres, therefore, use the most sophisticated computers and processing systems.

Vulnerability of main battle tanks

Weapon systems based on anti-tank, anti-aircraft and anti-ship missiles are particularly benefitting from the new technologies. New anti-tank missiles, for example, are rapidly making the main battle tank obsolete, particularly when used on helicopters.

Tanks face a number of threats, including: scatterable anti-tank mines; fixed mines, particularly smart ones; smart sub-munitions; and anti-tank missiles. Perhaps the most effective anti-tank operation is to funnel invading tanks into particular areas by minefields and anti-tank barriers, and then attack them with anti-tank missiles and cannons.

Anti-tank missiles are, therefore, an important (if not crucial) element in the defence against tank attack. Doubts about the future effectiveness of light short-range infantry anti-tank missiles have increased the importance of larger-diameter helicopter-borne anti-tank weapons. These doubts have arisen because of the introduction of explosive armour as extra protection for main battle tanks.

Explosive armour is undoubtedly a considerable problem for infantry anti-tank missiles, all of which use high-energy anti-tank (HEAT) warheads. HEAT warheads use chemical, rather than kinetic, energy in a shaped charge; a cone-shaped metal liner inside the warhead focuses energy on the target tank. A detonator on the nose of the warhead detonates a chemical high-explosive charge at a predetermined distance from the tank. The explosion produces a concentrated jet of molten metal which travels at some 9,000 metres a second. A metal plug, fired from the warhead, travels with the jet, and both penetrate the armour of the tank. The idea is that a stream of molten metal and hot gases enters the tank through the hole and fills the space inside the tank. This may kill, or disable, the crew directly or explode the ammunition in the tank.

Active explosive armour consists of 'bricks' of explosive, fastened to the tank's armour, sandwiched between two metal plates. If the tank is attacked by a HEAT warhead, the jet of the shaped charge detonates the explosive-armour brick, driving the plates apart. This disturbs the jet, reducing its effectiveness to penetrate the tank's armour.

Reactive explosive armour, a development of active explosive armour, anticipates the arrival of the HEAT warhead and detonates an appropriate 'brick' at a predetermined time before the warhead hits the tank, providing a greater disturbance of the jet of the shaped charge. Reactive explosive armour relies for its effectiveness, therefore, on its ability to detect the in-coming warhead in a timely way.

The advantage of explosive armour is that it is simple and cheap and can be retrofitted rapidly. It should be emphasized that explosive armour is effective only against some HEAT warheads, particularly those on man-portable infantry anti-tank missiles. Larger-diameter helicopter-launched HEAT warheads – such as those carried by Hellfire, HOT 2, Milan 2 and TOW 2 – still have a high (though reduced) kill probability because explosive armour reduces the penetration power of a shaped-charge warhead rather than totally destroying it. Explosive armour does not affect anti-tank warheads and armour-piercing ammunition that rely on kinetic energy.

Incidentally, it should be noted that if infantrymen could be trained to attack the weak points of a tank, i.e., not to concentrate only on the frontal arc, their anti-tank missiles would be effective even if the tank is equipped with explosive armour. One counter-measure to explosive armour would, therefore, be to retrain infantrymen in anti-tank techniques. But this is much easier said than done. It takes a brave infantryman to let enemy tanks pass him by so that he can attack them from the side or the rear!

Modern main battle tanks – such as the British Challenger, the German Leopard 2 and the American M1A1 Abrams – do not use explosive armour but rely on modern laminated and spaced armour, such as Chobham armour, to protect the tank against frontal attack. The thickness (and slope) of the armour protects against kinetic energy attack, and the laminations and air gaps of Chobham armour disturb the molten jet of shaped-charge warheads. Another new armour, for the M1A1 Abrams, uses depleted uranium (one of the densest materials available) encased in steel.

Anti-tank missile developments

Measures to improve the effectiveness of anti-tank missiles include the use of 'tandem' warheads. In one version, used on TOW 2A, a small shaped charge is used in a probe to detonate an explosive-armour brick at the optimum distance. The main warhead can then penetrate the tank's armour. Similar systems are used on HOT 2 and Milan 2. Typically, such warheads are larger, with weights increased from about 3 kilograms to about 6 kilograms.

Missiles under development (like the TOW 2B) will be provided with two 'proper' warheads, one clearing the way for the other. The obvious Russian counter-measure to tandem warheads is to use two thicknesses of explosive armour by overlapping or superimposing bricks; this is already being done.

Tandem warheads are, in any case, not the answer for infantry anti-tank missiles because they increase the weight and size of the missile beyond those acceptable in man-portable weapons. It is, in fact, difficult to see how these weapons can be made effective for the *frontal attack* of tanks protected with explosive armour.

A much more promising approach is to attack the turret of the tank, known as top attack. Because the turret has to rotate relatively rapidly, there is a limit to its weight and, therefore, to the thickness of the armour that can be used on it. Even though explosive armour can be used on the turret, the relative thinness of the underlying armour still makes it a weak spot. Also, in a top attack, the jet from the shaped charge strikes the armour perpendicularly, which reduces the effectiveness of explosive armour.

A tandem-warhead approach is proposed for the French–German– British TRIGAT missile programme and the American Anti-Armor Weapon System – Medium (AAWS–M). The USA is investigating three different technologies for an advanced, light, multi-purpose anti-tank missile (to replace Dragon). One uses a laser-beam-riding guidance system. The top-attack tandem warheads are fused to detonate at the optimum time to do maximum damage to the tank. The second approach uses fibre-optics guidance and an infra-red imager to acquire the target. (Incidentally, fibre-optics guidance is a powerful technique, potentially useful for very long range – tens of kilometres – missiles.)

The third approach is the most complex and expensive but potentially the most effective. It is based on a fire-and-forget missile which is locked on to the target before launch. A focal-plane infra-red seeker acquires the target. Once the seeker is locked on and the missile launched, it guides itself automatically to the target so that the operator can engage another target.

The TRIGAT (third generation anti-tank missile) programme includes a medium-range (up to 2 kilometres) infantry-portable missile (weighing 16 kilograms) to replace Milan and a long-range (up to 5 kilometres) helicopter- or ground-launched missile to replace HOT, Swingfire and TOW. The medium-range system is likely to use technologies very similar to those planned for the first American approach, based on laser beam riding and a tandem forward-facing warhead detonated at the optimum stand-off distance by a laser proximity fuse. The long-range system will probably be similar to the third American approach using an infra-red homing seeker and automatic target-tracking (i.e., it is a fire-and-forget system) so that an operator can engage several (probably four) targets simultaneously. The warhead will also be of the forward-facing tandem design.

The world's most sophisticated attack helicopter is the American Apache AH–64, armed with laser-guided Hellfire missiles. The Apache costs about $10 million; a laser Hellfire anti-tank missile costs about $45,000; and a typical main battle tank costs about $2.5 million. Operational research shows that one helicopter should, in battle, be able to destroy seventeen times its value in tanks before being shot down, and this excludes the cost of supporting and maintaining the tanks. For tanks in an anti-tank role, the ratio is considerably less than the 1:17 ratio for helicopters.

The use of fire-and-forget, top-attack, precision-guided missiles will allow the helicopter to attack from much larger ranges and considerably reduce its vulnerability. And so will improved avionics, allowing helicopters to operate at night and in bad weather.

New technologies will eventually revolutionize helicopters themselves. With today's design, the top speed of helicopters is limited to 400 kilometres per hour or so. Using technologies such as the Advancing Blade Concept (with two contra-rotating stiff rotors), Tilt Rotor (in which the rotors tilt through a right angle to provide lift or thrust or a combination of both) and the X wing, very much higher top speeds, even supersonic speeds, will become possible. Helicopters will then acquire new battlefield roles.

Non-offensive defence

In the face of developments in anti-tank warfare, main battle tanks are no longer cost-effective weapon systems. Anti-aircraft systems (such as the Patriot missile system) and anti-ship missiles are making long-range combat aircraft and large warships even more vulnerable than heavy tanks. The new military technologies are, therefore, making defence increasingly cost-effective in that it is cheaper to destroy long-range weapon systems like main battle tanks, long-range combat aircraft and large warships (seen to be the main weapons of invasion and occupation) than to deploy them. Put simply, today's most cost-effective weapons are short-range missiles designed to attack tanks, aircraft and warships. These missiles are cost-effective mainly because the cost of a missile is roughly proportional to the square of its range. For this reason, interest in military policies which emphasize defensive systems – called non-offensive or non-provocative defence – is increasing.

Non-offensive defence is, or very soon will be, the most cost-effective military posture. Non-offensive defence relies on the principle that the size, structure, weapons, logistics, training, manoeuvres, war games, military academy text-books, and all the other activities of the military forces can be so designed as to demonstrate *in their totality* that they provide an effective conventional defence but have virtually no offensive capability. The military forces could, on request, be opened for inspection by neighbouring or other countries to assure them of the non-aggressive, non-threatening nature of the forces.

Schemes for non-offensive defence vary in their details but have in common reliance on new cost-effective short-range missiles against attack by main battle tanks, combat aircraft and warships, and in-depth defence using a network of protected positions, decentralized and hence less vulnerable to attack and destruction. They also usually emphasize the need for well-fortified borders, using a variety of modern tank-barriers, the deployment of rapid earth-moving equipment, the use of anti-tank minefields with intelligence mines, and so on.

Critics often claim that conventional defensive deterrence uses only complex and highly centralized technologies. This is not so. Weapons and technologies would be chosen for specific tasks and operated well within their design characteristics. Emphasis would be given to simply operated and expendable missiles, cheap to produce in large quantities. But there would be a judicious mix of anti-tank missiles, anti-tank mines and anti-tank cannon; anti-aircraft missiles and light anti-aircraft guns; and direct and indirect fire.

The defence – including command, control and communications

centres – could be decentralized and would, therefore, not provide obvious targets for enemy bombardment. This is particularly true for a defensive system based on comparatively small, independent units armed with short-range weapons. With a larger number of cheap systems, there would be more redundancy and less scope for error.

Short-range systems also have the advantage of choice of weapons. Short-range missiles can be guided by laser, active or passive radar, infra-red, millimetre waves, fibre optics, etc. Mines can be fitted with various sensors – seismic, magnetic, acoustic, infra-red and so on. Choice increases the scope for surprise and further increases the effectiveness of the defence.

The advocates of conventional defensive deterrence have yet to convince military and defence establishments that the concept offers the most cost-effective defence. The lag between military technological advances and military tactics and bureaucratic inertia is a barrier to the adoption of a security policy based on a non-offensive defence, which is seen by many as a radical change. Traditionalists still cling to the outdated belief that 'offence is the best defence'.

Criteria for judging change in security policy

The criteria by which the effectiveness of a change of defence policy should be judged can be summarized as follows:

It should provide the most cost-effective defence within the military money available.
It should be militarily credible.
It should increase 'crisis stability', i.e., reduce the risk of a crisis degenerating into war.
It should decrease the pressure for an arms race.
It should improve the climate for arms control.
It should complement and enhance foreign policy.
It should be acceptable to public opinion.
It should be affordable.

Judged by these criteria, a new European security system should be based on a defensive military posture. In particular, the democratization process in eastern European countries and the former Soviet republics would be greatly assisted if the military postures of western European countries were demonstrably defensive. Moves to a non-offensive defence would, therefore, complement and enhance the foreign policy of western European countries.

Political leaders in both eastern and western Europe and the former Soviet republics, spurred on by the need for a new defence policy appropriate to a new European security system and by economic constraints, may well be anxious to negotiate mutual non-provocative defence strategies, with adequate verification, as part of the European disarmament process. If so, they will be in tune with military technological realities.

3

ARMS PRODUCTION AND TRADE

The 1991 Gulf War focused attention yet again on the morality and wisdom of the arms trade. Saddam Hussein imported virtually all the conventional weapons he used to fight his wars with Iran and Kuwait. Some forty countries sold weapons to Iran and Iraq during their war, some of them selling weapons to both sides. Without the arms trade, Saddam Hussein could not have become a significant military power.

The arms trade fuels regional arms races. Whether or not these arms races are a direct cause of war is not known. But it is certain that, once conflict breaks out, the sophisticated weapons acquired through the arms trade considerably increase the level of conflict. Almost all of the 200 or so wars fought since the Second World War have been fought with weapons imported from the industrialized countries.

Some 20 million people have been killed in these wars. The arms-sellers must take some responsibility for these deaths. Countries with even the most appalling human rights records have no difficulty buying weapons abroad, including weapons used to quell public protests and demonstrations.

The arms trade is unwise because weapons sold to other countries may be used against one's own troops. For example, the UK sold many major weapons and much military equipment to Argentina before the Falklands War. Many of the British servicemen killed in the war were killed by British weapons. Similarly, some of the coalition servicemen killed during the Gulf War were killed by weapons supplied by one or other coalition country.

Arms producers

The number of countries producing arms has been steadily increasing since the Second World War. In 1945, only five countries – Canada, Sweden, the USA, the USSR and the UK – had the capacity to develop and manufacture major weapons. Today, over fifty countries do so. (The most detailed information about the global arms trade is published by the Stockholm International Peace Research Institute. An annual arms trade register is published in the SIPRI yearbook. The information about the arms trade in this chapter comes mainly from SIPRI sources.)

The main industrialized arms-producing countries are: China, France, Germany, Italy, Japan, the Netherlands, Spain, Sweden, Switzerland, the UK, the USA and the former Soviet Union. The main arms producers in the Third World are: Argentina, Brazil, India, Israel, North Korea, South Africa, South Korea and Taiwan. Two of the hundred largest arms-producing companies are Indian, two are Israeli, one is Brazilian, one is South African and one is South Korean.

The top eight Third World arms-producing countries produce some 90 per cent of total Third World major-weapon production (Brzoska and Ohlson 1986). Another eighteen Third World countries produce some types of major weapon. Whereas the top eight industrialized arms producers make nearly 600 types of major weapon (about 230 types of aircraft, 70 types of armoured vehicle, 150 missiles and 150 warships), the top eight Third World producers make some 140 types of major weapon (about 65 types of aircraft, 15 types of armoured vehicle, 30 missiles and 30 warships).

Regional arms producers

Of the Middle Eastern countries, for example, Algeria indigenously designs and produces warships; Egypt indigenously designs and produces helicopters, strike aircraft, armoured vehicles, surface-to-air and anti-tank missiles, and warships; Iran indigenously designs and produces helicopters; and Israel indigenously designs and produces transport aircraft, multi-role combat aircraft, fighter aircraft, armoured vehicles including main battle tanks, and warships.

In addition, a variety of weapons are produced in the Middle East under licence from other countries. Egypt produces aircraft under licence from Brazil and France, anti-tank missiles under licence from the UK, and main battle tanks and surveillance radar under licence from the USA; Iran produces surface-to-surface missiles under licence from China; and Jordan produces helicopters under licence from the USA.

Israel's armaments industry is large enough to sell significant amounts of weapons abroad: air-to-air missiles to Argentina; ship-to-ship missiles, surface-to-air missiles and missile-armed fast patrol boats to Chile; multi-role combat aircraft and ship-to-air missiles to Colombia; fast patrol boats to Sri Lanka; air-to-air missiles to Thailand; and transport aircraft to Venezuela. Israel has issued licences to Belgium to produce Israeli battlefield radar and to the USA to produce point defence radar and air-to-surface missiles. Iran is trying to export a variety of artillery rockets.

Egypt, Iran and Israel have stated their intention to continue to develop their arms industries. In particular, they intend to develop military electronics programmes. But neither the Arab countries nor Iran can yet produce large quantities of major weapons; nor can they produce very sophisticated weapons. Israel, on the other hand, produces very sophisticated weapons – such as the Kfir multi-role combat aircraft – which compete with the most sophisticated American weapons. There is, therefore, a considerable imbalance between the arms-production capabilities of the Arab countries and those of Israel.

It should be noted that attempts to restrict the development of Iranian and Iraqi arms industries during the Iran–Iraq War by denying them components failed dismally. It is hard to believe that efforts to restrict the development of indigenous Middle East arms industries during peacetime will be any more successful. We must expect Arab arms industries to expand steadily. But the imbalance between them and Israeli arms industries will remain for the foreseeable future. The Arab countries will want to continue to redress the balance by buying arms abroad.

Argentina and Brazil are the main arms producers in Latin America. Argentina produces a variety of military aircraft including trainers and counter-insurgency aircraft; armoured vehicles, including armoured personnel-carriers and tanks; air-to-surface missiles and anti-tank missiles; and warships, including frigates and submarines. Brazil produces helicopters, trainers, transport aircraft, counter-insurgency aircraft and marine patrol aircraft; armoured vehicles, including armoured personnel-carriers; air-to-air missiles, air-to-surface missiles and anti-tank missiles; and warships, including frigates and submarines.

The main Asian Third World arms-producers are India, North Korea, South Korea and Taiwan. India produces a variety of aircraft, including helicopters, transport aircraft, counter-insurgency aircraft, trainer aircraft and fighters; armoured vehicles, including armoured personnel-carriers and main battle tanks; missiles, including air-to-air missiles and anti-tank missiles; and warships, including destroyers and submarines. North Korea produces main battle tanks and small warships. South Korea produces helicopters, fighter aircraft, armoured personnel-vehicles, submarines and small warships. Taiwan produces fighter and trainer aircraft, armoured personnel-vehicles, surface-to-surface missiles, ship-to-ship missiles, anti-tank missiles and small warships.

South Africa produces a range of armoured vehicles, including armoured cars and armoured personnel-carriers; missiles, including air-to-air missiles; and small warships.

Domestic arms production is encouraged by the increasing tendency of the main suppliers to manipulate arms supplies for political, economic or military reasons. Countries like South Africa and Taiwan have found it so hard to buy weapons that they have decided to produce their own. Countries like Israel refuse to depend on others, even if they have dependable suppliers.

Who buys and sells weapons?

Of the $1,000,000 million given each year to the world's military, some $250,000 million goes on buying weapons. Producing and selling weapons is the world's second-biggest industry, after oil (which, for comparison, grosses roughly $430,000 million a year). Of the weapons produced by the world's weapons industries, about $60,000 million worth are traded annually in the global arms market.

The SIPRI arms trade registers show that in the past five years no less than 132 countries (out of the total of about 160 countries in the world) imported major conventional weapons (armoured vehicles, missiles, combat aircraft and warships) (SIPRI 1991). The USA exported major weapons to 77 countries, France exported major weapons to 73 countries, the UK to 49 countries, the USSR to 38 countries, Italy to 35 countries, China to 22 countries, Germany to 31 countries, the Netherlands to 15 countries, Sweden to 11 countries and Czechoslovakia to 10 countries.

Arms exporters

The former Soviet Union and the USA have been the biggest arms traders, together supplying about 70 per cent of the major weapons sold abroad. The Soviet Union accounted for about 38 per cent of the global arms trade during the past five years; the USA accounted for about 31 per cent. The second-rank arms traders are France, which accounted for about 9 per cent of the global trade in major weapons during the past five years; the UK, which accounted for about 4 per cent; China, about 4 per cent; and Germany, about 3 per cent. These six arms exporters account for about 90 per cent of the global arms trade during the past five years.

Where do the exported weapons go? There has been a major change in the pattern of arms sales in recent years (Anthony *et al.* 1991). The industrialized countries are increasingly important arms-importers. The share of the rich countries in the global arms trade has increased from about 33 per cent in 1987 to 50 per cent in 1989. Increased imports by Japan and – despite the end of the Cold War – the NATO countries mainly account for this trend.

Third World countries are less inclined to buy arms because of the debt crisis, declining oil prices, the ending of some significant wars (such as the Iran–Iraq War and the fighting in Angola) and the expansion of some Third World domestic arms industries.

The former Soviet Union sold most major weapons to the Third World during the past five years, accounting for about 44 per cent of the weapons sold. The USA accounted for about 20 per cent of sales of major weapons to the Third World; France accounted for about 11 per cent; China for about 6 per cent; and the UK for about 5 per cent. The other significant suppliers were Germany, Italy, the Netherlands, Brazil and Israel, together accounting for about 7 per cent of the total. These top ten suppliers accounted for about 93 per cent of the major weapons sold to the Third World during the past five years.

The top ten suppliers of major weapons to the industrialized countries during the past five years were: the USA (about 47 per cent); the former Soviet Union (about 30 per cent); France (about 5 per cent); Germany (about 5 per cent); the UK (about 3 per cent); Czechoslovakia (about 3 per cent); Sweden (about 1.5 per cent); Canada (about 1.5 per cent); Poland (about 0.7 per cent); and Italy (about 0.6 per cent). These ten suppliers account for about 97 per cent of the major weapons sold to the industrialized countries during the past five years.

About 80 per cent of Soviet arms exports over the past five years went to nine countries: Afghanistan, Angola, Czechoslovakia, East Germany, India, Iraq, North Korea, Poland and Syria. Japan, Spain, Egypt, Saudi Arabia, South Korea, West Germany and Israel were America's main customers. Saudi Arabia, India, Iraq and the United Arab Emirates were France's main customers. And Saudi Arabia and India were Britain's main customers.

It should be noted that in 1990 the value of Soviet arms exports sharply decreased. Compared to earlier years it roughly halved and, for the first time for nearly a decade, the Soviet Union took second place to the USA in the rank order of arms exporters. In 1990, I. S. Belousov, Deputy Chairman of the Council of Ministers of the USSR, stated that Soviet weapon exports had been much reduced during the current five-year plan. Missiles, he said, were reduced by 64 per cent, ships by 56 per cent, aircraft by 53 per cent, artillery by 48 per cent, and tanks and armoured personnel-carriers by 25–30 per cent. The longer-term contribution of the former Soviet Union to the global arms trade is impossible to predict or even speculate about.

Arms importers

A relatively few countries are the main importers of arms. The four leading importers – India, Japan, Saudi Arabia and Iraq – accounted for 30 per cent of the major weapons transferred during the past five years. The next six leading importers – Afghanistan, Czechoslovakia, Egypt, North Korea, Poland and Spain – accounted for another 20 per cent. The next five importers – Angola, Greece, South Korea, Syria and Turkey – accounted for another 11 per cent, so that the top fifteen importers accounted for nearly two-thirds of the major weapons transferred abroad.

In the industrialized countries, the major importers of major weapons during the past five years were: Japan (accounting for about 16 per cent of the total), Czechoslovakia (about 8 per cent), Spain (about 8 per cent), Turkey (about 7 per cent), Poland (about 7 per cent), Canada (about 5 per cent) and Greece (about 5 per cent). These seven countries account for about 56 per cent of the total imports of major weapons into industrialized countries. Seven other countries (Germany, Australia, the Netherlands, the former Soviet Union, Bulgaria, Hungary and Yugoslavia) account for about another 25 per cent.

In the Third World, the leading importers of major weapons during the past five years were India (accounting for about 16 per cent of the total), Iraq (about 11 per cent), Saudi Arabia (about 8 per cent), Syria (about 6 per cent), Egypt (about 5 per cent), North Korea (about 5 per cent) and Afghanistan (about 4 per cent). These seven countries account for about 56 per cent of the total. Angola, Libya, Taiwan, Iran, Pakistan, South Korea and Israel together account, roughly equally, for about another 20 per cent.

Within the Third World, the Middle East is by far the most active importing region. During the past five years, for example, about 41 per cent of the major weapons transferred to the Third World went to the Middle East. South-East Asia accounts for about another 24 per cent; the Far East accounts for 16 per cent; Africa for 11 per cent; and Latin America for 8 per cent. In the next few years, the countries of the Indian sub-continent and South-East Asia are expected to increase their share.

Why do countries buy and sell weapons?

The motives for selling weapons vary. The USA has done so mainly to gain political or economic influence in Third World regions or to acquire military bases abroad. The former Soviet Union had similar motives. The smaller suppliers believe that arms sales help their economies, particularly in times of recession.

A most important factor is that the major powers can afford to buy appropriate quantities of major weapons for their own arsenals only if they achieve the economies of scale to be had from long production-runs. By selling weapons abroad countries reduce the costs of those same weapons for their own armed forces. Maintaining and increasing arms sales is, therefore, crucially important for the governments of the major exporters of weapons.

Pressure to export weapons will increase as military budgets in the USA, the former Soviet Union, and eastern and western Europe decrease as the Cold War ends. Arms industries will look to exports to increase sales as domestic orders decrease. Domestic orders alone will, for many arms companies, be insufficient to allow them to survive. Also, companies want to recover the enormous research-and-development costs involved in designing and building modern weapons.

For these reasons, commercial firms apply considerable political pressure on governments to persuade them to grant export licences for their wares. Many governments are only too willing to comply. Often civil servants from the major arms suppliers ply their wares abroad. In the UK, for example, the Defence Sales Organization in the Ministry of Defence energetically promotes British arms exports and, in France, the Directorate for International Affairs in the Defence Ministry has the same promotional task.

The dismal failure of previous attempts at controlling the global arms trade – such as President Carter's programme of restraint, announced in May 1977, and the Soviet–American Conventional Arms Transfer Talks in the late 1970s – demonstrate the power and effectiveness of the vested interests – industrial and governmental – in the industrialized countries intent on maintaining and increasing the lucrative arms trade.

The sale of arms is used by the major powers to retain and expand political influence in a given region. Supplying weapons is seen by the major arms suppliers as a way of achieving this foreign-policy goal. There are also resource-related motives for selling weapons to certain Third World regions. To ensure oil supplies, for example, is an obvious reason for supplying weapons to Middle Eastern governments.

The motives for buying arms also vary. Some countries do so because they have real, or perceived, security needs. Arms are seen to be needed to deal with internal or external conflicts in which military force may be required. A vicious circle may then be established. When one country acquires sophisticated weapons its neighbours may feel threatened and will want similar weapons. An arms race then begins.

Third World countries with military governments are particularly good customers for arms. Military leaders usually want the most sophisticated weapons because they are the most glamorous. Other Third World governments need the political support of senior military officers and can get this support only by satisfying the military demands for the latest weaponry. Some countries – such as Israel –

have a sublime faith in the superiority of technology, including military technology, and feel secure only when their arsenals contain the most sophisticated weapons.

The latter motive for importing weapons has been enhanced by the experience of the Gulf War. The systematic destruction of Iraq by high-technology weapons, and Iraq's inability to respond, left few in doubt about the overwhelming superiority of the military technology of the industrialized powers. The war demonstrated for all to see that recent advances in military technology have given the military extraordinary new capabilities. Other countries are anxious to acquire these capabilities by buying high-technology weapons.

4

THE PROLIFERATION OF BALLISTIC MISSILES

The Gulf War heightened concern over the global spread of sophistica-ted weapon-delivery systems. But there is most concern about the proliferation of missiles, particularly ballistic missiles, enhanced by Iraqi Scud surface-to-surface missile attacks on Israel and on coalition forces in Saudi Arabia.

Ballistic missiles are ideal systems for delivering weapons of mass destruction, particularly over long distances. In fact, given the cost of ballistic missiles and the relatively small payloads they carry, it is hardly worth acquiring them just to deliver conventional warheads.

Not only are more countries acquiring missiles through the global arms trade, but several Third World countries are also able to design and manufacture them indigenously. The more producers there are, the easier it is to acquire missiles, either in the global arms trade or illegally. Currently, twenty Third World countries either possess ballis-tic missiles or are trying to develop them. These are Algeria, Argen-tina, Brazil, Egypt, Greece, India, Iran, Iraq, Israel, Kuwait, Libya, North Korea, Pakistan, Saudi Arabia, South Africa, South Korea, South Yemen, Syria, Taiwan and Turkey (Karp 1991).

It is not unreasonable to worry about the possibility that sub-national groups will, in the future, acquire and use ballistic missiles as delivery systems for weapons of mass destruction. This risk is obviously enhanced if significant numbers of ballistic missiles are deployed by many countries.

The extent to which ballistic-missile production has already spread into Third World countries is shown in Table 4.1 (Karp 1991). The Third World countries producing short-range missiles are shown in Table 4.2. Imported ballistic missiles in service are shown in Table 4.3.

Before the Gulf War, Iraq was making rapid progress in the develop-ment of several types of ballistic missile. North Korea has shown significant expertise in ballistic-missile development. Not only is it manufacturing Russian Scud missiles but it is also developing the Scud-PIP (Scud Product Improvement Programme), having a

Table 4.1 Ballistic missiles under development or being produced in the Third World

Range	40–150 km	150–600 km	over 600 km
Brazil	EE-150 SS-60 X-40	SS-300	
Egypt	Saqr-80 Scud 100		Badr-2000
India		Prithvi	Agni
Indonesia	RX-250		
Iran	Oghab Shanin-2 Nazeat		
Iraq	Laith Ababil 50 Sijeel 60 Ababil 100	al-Hussein Fahd	al-Abbas Condor 2 Tamuz-1
Israel	MAR-350	Jericho I	Jericho II
Libya			Ittisalt
North Korea	Scud B	Scud PIP	
Pakistan	Hatf-2	Hatf-1	
Saudi Arabia	SS-60		
South Africa			Jericho II
Taiwan	Ching Feng		
Thailand	Thanu Fan		

Table 4.2 Short-range missiles produced in Third World countries

	Designation	Missile type
Argentina	Martin Pescador	anti-tank
	Mathago	anti-tank
Brazil	Pirhana	air-to-air
	Carcara	air-to-surface
Israel	Barak	surface-to-air
	Gabriel-1/2/3	ship-to-ship
	Gabriel-3A/S	air-to-ship
	Picket	anti-tank
	Python-3	air-to-air
	Shafrir-2	air-to-air
Taiwan	Kun Wu	anti-tank

maximum range of about 500 kilometres. This development is note-worthy because North Korea is reported to have developed chemical warheads for its ballistic missiles and is suspected of developing nuclear weapons.

Some Third World countries are developing sounding rockets, for use in researching the properties of the upper atmosphere, and space-launch vehicles, to put satellites into orbit. Both of these technologies

Table 4.3 Other surface-to-surface ballistic missiles in service in Third World countries

	Designation	Range (km)	Supplier
Afghanistan	Scud B	280	USSR
Algeria	FROG-7	70	USSR
Cuba	FROG-4	50	USSR
	FROG-7	70	USSR
Egypt	Scud B	280	USSR
	FROG-5	50	USSR
	FROG-7	70	USSR
Iran	Scud B	280	USSR
Iraq	Scud B	280	USSR
	FROG-7	70	USSR
	SS-60	60	Brazil
Israel	Lance	120	USA
North Korea	FROG-5	50	USSR
	FROG-7	70	USSR
South Korea	Honest John	37	USA
	Nike Hercules	240	USA
Kuwait	FROG-7	70	USSR
Libya	Scud B	280	USSR
	FROG-7	70	USSR
	M-9	600	China
Saudi Arabia	CSS-2	2700	China
	SS-60	60	Brazil
Syria	Scud B	280	USSR
	FROG-7	70	USSR
	SS-21 Scarab	120	USSR
	M-9	600	China
Taiwan	Honest John	37	USA
Turkey	Honest John	37	USA
Yemen	Scud B	280	USSR
	FROG-7	70	USSR
	SS-21 Scarab	120	USSR

provide countries with the capability to produce long-range ballistic missiles. The rockets used in these civilian activities are, in fact, basically similar to military missiles.

Brazil, India and Pakistan have each developed two types of sounding rockets; and Indonesia is developing one type. Israel has developed a space-launch vehicle and has actually launched two satellites into orbit. Brazil, India and Taiwan are developing space-launch vehicles. South Korea and Pakistan plan to do so.

India and Israel are making steady progress with their missile programmes. But in the other countries ballistic-missile programmes have been slowed or stopped altogether. Argentina's Condor programme, for example, has been shelved but it could be restarted in the future.

5

THE NUCLEAR DIMENSION

Nuclear weapons will remain of central importance in international affairs for the foreseeable future, even though the size of the main nuclear arsenals will be reduced. Although the military budgets of the major industrialized countries will probably decrease in the coming years, the resources devoted by both the USA and possibly the Commonwealth of Independent States to research into and the development of nuclear weapons and their delivery systems is unlikely to decrease.

Many Russians, particularly the military and defence bureaucrats, believe that the superpower status of Russia depends mainly on the maintenance of a strategic nuclear force and the continual modernization of this force. The USA believes fundamentally that its national security depends on maintaining its position as world leader in military technology, including its leadership in nuclear-weapon technology.

We can, therefore, expect the east–west nuclear arms race to go on for a while, in spite of the break-up of the former Soviet Union and *détente*. Even though the risk of a deliberate global nuclear war may, in the words of Mikhail Gorbachev, have 'practically disappeared', the risk of nuclear war by accident will still be with us.

But perhaps the most serious nuclear threat arises from the spread of nuclear weapons to countries that do not now have them. Most believe that the more nuclear-weapon powers there are the greater the risk of nuclear war. A future war in an unstable region, such as the Middle East, which includes one or more countries with a nuclear force may escalate to a nuclear war involving nuclear-weapon powers outside the region. Such a war may begin with conventional weapons and then escalate to a local nuclear war in which the nuclear weapons of local powers are used. This local nuclear war may then spread, say, to Europe. There is then an obvious link between the proliferation of nuclear forces and world security.

A third nuclear threat is nuclear terrorism, to be dealt with in detail in Chapter 7. There is a considerable risk that sub-national groups, including terrorists and even small groups of criminals, will in the future acquire fissile material – particularly plutonium – and construct a nuclear explosive. Nuclear terrorism has considerable ramifications for world, as well as regional, security. Any use of nuclear explosives could escalate to a nuclear world war.

To understand the extent of these nuclear threats to world security it is useful to begin by briefly considering the nature of nuclear explosives.

Nuclear explosives

The design of a 'first generation' nuclear weapon, such as the bomb that destroyed Nagasaki in 1945, is no longer secret. Amory B. Lovins, for example, in an article in the scientific journal *Nature*, summarized the bulk of the necessary physics data showing that a component nuclear physicist can find the relevant information in the open literature (Lovins 1980).

Fission weapons

The basic nuclear weapon is the fission weapon, or A-bomb (A for atomic) as it was first called. A fission chain reaction is used to produce a very large amount of energy in a very short time – roughly a millionth of a second – and therefore a very powerful explosion.

The fission occurs in an isotope of a heavy element – either uranium or plutonium. Specifically, the fission bombs built so far have used the isotopes uranium-235 or plutonium-239 as the fissile material. A fission occurs when a neutron (one of nature's elementary particles) enters the nucleus of an atom of one of these materials, which then breaks up or 'fissions'.

When a fission occurs a large amount of energy is released; the original nucleus is split into two radioactive nuclei, the fission products; and two or three neutrons are released. These neutrons can be used to produce a self-sustaining chain reaction. A chain reaction will take place if at least one of the neutrons released in each fission event goes on to produce the fission of another uranium or plutonium nucleus.

There exists a critical mass for uranium-235 and plutonium-239 – the smallest amount of the material in which a self-sustaining chain reaction is just sustained. The critical mass is that from which just as many neutrons escape per unit time as are released by fission. If this mass of material is increased, the number of neutrons produced by fission builds up, and considerably more fissions occur in each successive generation. A 'super-critical' mass is created and a nuclear explosion takes place.

The critical mass depends on a number of factors. First, the nuclear properties of the material used for the fission, whether it is uranium-235 or plutonium-239. Second, the shape of the material – a sphere is the optimum shape because for a given mass the surface area is minimized which, in turn, minimizes the number of neutrons escaping through the surface per unit time and thereby lost to the fission process. Third, the density of the material (the higher the density, the shorter the average distance travelled by a neutron before causing another fission and therefore the smaller the critical mass). Fourth, the purity of the material (if materials other than the one used for fission are present, some neutrons may be captured by their nuclei instead of causing fission). Fifth, the physical surrounding of the material used for fission (if the material is surrounded by a medium like beryllium, which reflects neutrons back into the material, some of the reflected neutrons may be used for fission which would otherwise have been lost, thus reducing the critical mass).

The critical mass of, for example, a sphere of pure plutonium-239 metal in its densest form (alpha-phase, density 19.8 grams per cubic centimetre) is about 10 kilograms. The radius of the sphere is about 5 centimetres. If the plutonium sphere is surrounded by a natural uranium neutron reflector, about 10 centimetres thick, the critical mass is reduced to about 4.4 kilograms, a sphere of a radius of about 3.6 centimetres. A 32-centimetre-thick beryllium reflector reduces the critical mass to about 2.5 kilograms, a sphere of a radius of 3.1 centimetres.

Using a cunning technique called implosion, in which conventional chemical explosives are used to produce a shock wave which uniformly compresses the plutonium sphere, the volume of the plutonium sphere can be slightly reduced and its density increased. If the original mass of the plutonium is just less than critical, it will, after compression, become super-critical and a nuclear explosion will take place.

Using implosion, a nuclear explosion could, with a good modern design including an effective, but practicable, reflector, be achieved with about 2.5 kilograms of plutonium. The trick is to obtain very uniform compression of the sphere.

In an implosion design, the plutonium would be surrounded by a spherical shell, made from a heavy metal, like natural uranium, which acts as the tamper. The conventional explosive used to compress the plutonium sphere is placed outside the tamper.

The tamper has two functions. First, because the tamper is made of heavy metal, its inertia helps hold together the plutonium during the explosion to prevent the premature disintegration of the fissioning material and thereby obtain a greater efficiency. Second, the tamper converts the divergent detonation wave into a convergent shock wave to compress the plutonium sphere.

The plutonium may also be surrounded by another spherical shell, situated between the plutonium and the tamper. Its purpose is to reflect back into the plutonium some of the neutrons which escaped through the surface of the plutonium core to minimize the mass of plutonium needed. Beryllium is a good neutron-reflecting material.

In a nuclear explosion exceedingly high temperatures (hundreds of millions of degrees centigrade) and exceedingly high pressures (millions of atmospheres) build up very rapidly (in about half a millionth of a second, the time taken for about fifty-five generations of fission). The mass of the material used for fission expands at very high speeds – initially at a speed of about 1,000 kilometres a second. In much less than a millionth of a second the size and density of the material have changed so that it becomes less than critical and the chain reaction stops. The designer of a nuclear weapon aims at keeping the fissionable material together, against its tendency to fly apart, long enough to produce an explosion powerful enough for his purpose.

The complete fission of 1 kilogram of plutonium-239 would produce an explosion equivalent to that of 18,000 tons (18 kilotons, or kt) of TNT. Modern fission bombs have efficiencies approaching 40 per cent, giving yields of 7 kilotons or so per kilogram of plutonium present. It is this high yield-to-weight ratio that makes nuclear weapons so special.

A major problem in designing implosion fission weapons for maximum efficiency is to prevent the chain reaction from being started before the maximum achievable super-criticality is reached – an eventuality called pre-detonation. Pre-detonation is most likely to be caused by a neutron from spontaneous fission – fission that occurs naturally without the stimulation of an external neutron – in the material used for fission. In 6 kilograms of plutonium-239, for example, the average time between spontaneous fissions is only about three-millionths of a second. To prevent pre-detonation and loss of efficiency, the assembly of a plutonium bomb must be very rapid. Implosion is necessary.

The timing of the detonations of the chemical explosives to produce the shock wave to compress the plutonium sphere is crucial for the efficient operation of an implosion atomic bomb. Microsecond (a millionth of a second) precision is essential. The shapes of the explosive lenses are rather complex and must be carefully calculated. The high explosive must be chemically extremely pure and of constant constituency throughout its volume.

The Nagasaki bomb used high-explosive charges of Composition B, a mixture of cyclotrimethylene-trinitramine (RDX) and trinitrotoluene (TNT), a fast-burning explosive more effective than TNT on its own.

More modern implosion charges use diaminotrinitrobenzene (DATB) or triaminotrinitrobenzine (TATB). The amount of high explosive used in a fission weapon has decreased considerably since 1945 – from about 500 kilograms to about 15 kilograms or less (Hansen 1988).

Normally, the more explosive charges there are, the more perfect is the spherical symmetry of the shock wave. Forty or so detonations would be typical. Getting the timing of the detonation sequence – milli-microsecond (a thousandth of a millionth of a second) precision is essential – and the chemistry and geometrical shapes of the explosive lenses right is the most difficult problem in designing an efficient implosion-type nuclear fission weapon.

A typical circuit to fire the detonators uses Krytrons to generate short high-current pulses with amplitudes of about 4,000 volts and rise-and-fall times of a few milli-microseconds. The Krytron is a cold-cathode gas-filled switch using an arc discharge to conduct high peak currents for short times.

The energy in the current pulse used to fire the detonators in a nuclear weapon is normally produced by charged capacitors. Because the rate of change of current is very large, the capacitors must have a very low self-inductance. This is why the manufacture of such capacitors, rugged enough for military use, requires special attention.

For maximum efficiency, the chain reaction in an atomic bomb must be initiated at precisely the right moment – the moment of maximum super-criticality. The initiation is achieved by a pulse of neutrons. In today's nuclear weapons, the neutron pulse is produced by a small electronic device called a neutron 'gun'. The problem of getting the timing of the shaped-charge detonations and the injection of the neutron pulse right is mainly theoretical, in calculating the timing sequence for optimum efficiency. The practical problems of manufacturing the electronic components and building the circuits to produce the calculated sequence of triggering pulses are much less difficult.

The alternative to plutonium-239 as the fissile material in a nuclear weapon is uranium-235, although some of the most advanced types of nuclear weapon contain both materials arranged in thin concentric shells, rather than a solid sphere. Plutonium undergoes fission faster than uranium, and placing it inside a shell of enriched uranium makes more efficient use of its fission neutrons. In this way a greater explosive power can be achieved for a given mass of fissile material.

The amount of highly enriched uranium in, for example, the American nuclear arsenal is about 500 tons, five times the amount of plutonium in the arsenal. But the more modern nuclear weapons tend to use relatively more plutonium than earlier models.

Natural uranium contains the isotopes uranium-235 and uranium-238. As dug out of the ground, uranium is mostly uranium-238 – out of a thousand atoms of natural uranium, only seven are uranium-235. The problem with uranium-238 is that a neutron can only cause fission in it if its velocity exceeds a certain value. But too few of the neutrons available from the fission process have more than this critical velocity to sustain a chain reaction. A chain reaction is, therefore, not possible using uranium-238. But a nucleus of uranium-235, like a nucleus of plutonium-239, will undergo fission when any neutron, even one moving very slowly, collides with it. And so a chain reaction is possible using uranium-235.

To obtain uranium that can be used to construct a nuclear weapon, the amount of uranium-235 in natural uranium is increased by a process called enrichment. The proportion of uranium-235 is normally enriched from its natural value of 0.7 per cent to more than 40 per cent, preferably to over 95 per cent. The greater the amount of uranium-235 in the uranium, the less will be the critical mass.

In uranium-235, the average time between spontaneous fissions is much greater than it is in plutonium-239, and the so-called 'gun' method can be used to assemble a critical mass of uranium-235 in a nuclear weapon. In the Hiroshima bomb, for example, a less than critical mass of uranium-235 was fired down a 'cannon barrel' (the barrel from a naval gun) into another less than critical mass of uranium-235 placed in front of the 'muzzle'. When the two masses came together they formed a super-critical mass which exploded.

About 60 kilograms of uranium-235 were used in the Hiroshima bomb. About 700 grams were fissioned. The average time between spontaneous fissions was about one-fiftieth of a second – quite adequate for the gun technique. The yield of the Hiroshima bomb was about 12.5 kt.

A fission weapon using uranium-235 can, however, also be made using the implosion technique. If surrounded by a reflector made from natural uranium 15 centimetres thick, 100 per cent pure uranium-235 has a critical mass of 15 kilograms (compared with 4.4 kilograms for plutonium-239). With uranium enriched to 40 per cent uranium-235, the critical mass increases to 75 kilograms; with 20 per cent uranium-235, it is 250 kilograms. High concentrations of uranium-235 are, therefore, very desirable if the material is to be used to produce nuclear weapons.

Designs based on the Hiroshima and Nagasaki bombs are likely to be used by countries beginning a nuclear-weapon programme. But even the first weapons now produced by a country would probably be more sophisticated than these early, primitive weapons. The Nagasaki bomb, for example, was about 3 metres long, 1.5 metres wide, and weighed about 4.5 tons. A modern fission weapon, even the first produced in a nuclear-weapon programme, should weigh no more than a few hundred kilograms.

The difficulty of designing and fabricating a nuclear weapon from earlier plutonium-239 or uranium-235 is often exaggerated. A competent group of nuclear physicists, and electronics and explosives engineers, given adequate resources and access to the literature, would have little difficulty in designing and constructing such a weapon from scratch. They would not need access to any classified literature.

Boosted fission weapons

Although very large explosions – equivalent to the explosion of 100 or 200 kt of TNT – can be obtained from nuclear weapons based on pure fission, there is a limit to the explosive power that can be obtained from an *operational* one. The maximum explosive power of a militarily usable fission weapon is 50 kt. Higher explosive power than can be achieved by a pure fission nuclear device can be obtained by 'boosting'.

In a boosted weapon, some fusion material is placed at the centre of the plutonium sphere in a fission weapon. When the fission weapon explodes, nuclear fusion takes place. The neutrons produced during the fusion process produce additional fissions in the plutonium in the weapon, increasing its efficiency. The fusion is used mainly as an additional source of neutrons to help the fission process, rather than as a direct source of energy.

Boosted weapons are essentially sophisticated fission weapons. Using boosting, a much higher explosive power is obtained from a given amount of plutonium. Militarily usable boosted weapons have explosive powers of 500 kt, i.e., about ten times the power of non-boosted operational weapons. The yields of the most powerful boosted weapons are equal to those of low-yield thermonuclear weapons.

In a typical boosted weapon a mixture of deuterium and tritium gases (heavy isotopes of hydrogen) is used as the fusion material. A pressurized deuterium–tritium mixture is injected from a reservoir, placed outside the fission-weapon core, into a space at the centre of the plutonium sphere after the fission process has begun. Because the centre of the sphere is needed for the fusion mixture, a boosted weapon must be initiated by an external neutron gun.

The pressure in the boosting system is typically about 20 million N per m², and about 5 grams of the deuterium – tritium gas mixture are injected into the centre of the plutonium sphere. The timing of the injection is crucial for maximum efficiency.

H-bombs

If explosions in the range of 1,000 kt, or 1 megaton (mt), are required, extra energy must be obtained from fusion. The fusion process is the opposite of fission. In fission, heavy nuclei are split into lighter ones. In fusion, light nuclei are formed (i.e., fused) into heavier nuclei.

In nuclear weapons, the heavier isotopes of hydrogen – deuterium and tritium – are fused to form helium. The fusion process, like the fission process, produces energy and is accompanied by the emission of neutrons. There is no critical mass for the fusion process; and, therefore, in theory, there is no limit to the explosive yield of fusion weapons – or H-bombs (H for hydrogen) as they are often called.

Fission is relatively easy to initiate – one neutron will start a chain reaction going in a critical mass of fissionable material, such as plutonium-239 or uranium-235. But fusion is possible only if the nuclei to be fused together are given a high enough energy to overcome the repulsive electric force between them due to their positive electric charges. In H-bombs, this energy is provided by raising the temperature of the fusion material. Because H-bombs depend on heat they are also called thermonuclear weapons.

In a typical thermonuclear weapon, deuterium and tritium are fused together. But to get this fusion reaction to work the deuterium–tritium mixture must be raised to a temperature of a hundred million degrees Centigrade or so. This can be provided only by a pure fission nuclear weapon (atomic bomb) in which such a temperature occurs at the moment of the explosion. An H-bomb, therefore, consists of a fission stage, which is an atomic bomb acting as a trigger, and a fusion stage, in which hydrogen isotopes (tritium and deuterium) are fused by the heat produced by the trigger.

Normally, the fusion material is in the form of a cylinder. The cylinder is made out of lithium deuteride. When neutrons from the fission explosion bombard lithium nuclei in the lithium deuteride, tritium nuclei are produced. The tritium nuclei fuse with deuterium nuclei in the lithium deuteride to produce fusion energy.

It is very advantageous to use lithium deuteride as the fusion material because it is a solid at normal temperatures whereas tritium and deuterium, the fusion materials used in boosted weapons, are gases at normal temperatures. It is, of course, much easier to construct nuclear weapons from solid materials than from gases.

The energy released from such a thermonuclear weapon comes from the fission trigger and the fusion material. But, if the fusion device is surrounded by a shell of uranium metal, the high-energy neutrons produced in the fusion process will cause additional fissions in the uranium shell. This technique can be used to enhance considerably the explosive power of a thermonuclear weapon. Such a weapon is called a fission–fusion–fission device. On average, about half of the yield from a typical thermonuclear weapon will come from fission and the other half from fusion.

H-bombs are much more difficult to design than fission nuclear weapons. The problem is to prevent the fission trigger from blowing the whole weapon apart before enough fusion material has been ignited to give the required explosive yield. Sufficient energy has to be delivered to the fusion material to start the thermonuclear reaction in a time much shorter than the time it takes for the explosion to occur. This means that the energy must be delivered with a speed approaching the speed of light.

Rotblat has described the technique used:

> The solution to the problem lies in the fact that at the very high temperature of the fission trigger most of the energy is emitted in the form of X-rays. These X-rays, travelling with the speed of light, radiate out from the centre and on reaching the tamper (surrounding the fusion material) are absorbed in it and then immediately re-emitted in the form of softer X-rays. By an appropriate configuration of the trigger and the fusion material it is possible to ensure that the X-rays reach the latter almost instantaneously. If the fusion material is sub-divided into small portions, each surrounded with a thin absorber made of a heavy metal, the bulk of the fusion material will simultaneously receive enough energy to start the thermonuclear reaction before the explosion disperses the whole assembly.
>
> (Rotblat 1981)

Although essentially weightless, X-rays can exert great pressure. In an H-bomb, the pressure (several million pounds per square inch) is exerted uniformly on the fusion material and long enough for the fusion process to work before the material is blown apart. Because the radiation travels at the speed of light, it arrives at the fusion material about a millionth of a second before the much slower moving shock wave from the trigger explosion. When the shock wave arrives, and blows the assembly apart, the fusion explosion has occurred.

The fusion process in a thermonuclear weapon is initiated by a so-called 'sparkplug', a thin sub-critical cylindrical rod of weapons-grade uranium-235 or plutonium-239 placed at the centre of the cylinder of fusion fuel (Hansen 1988). When the fusion fuel has been compressed, by radiation from the explosion of the fission trigger, neutrons from the trigger penetrate into the sparkplug. The sparkplug begins to fission; and the fission reaction, in the middle of the highly compressed fusion fuel, initiates the main fusion explosion.

Very large explosive yields have been obtained with thermonuclear weapons. Typically, each stage of a thermonuclear explosion explodes with a power roughly ten times that of the preceding stage. If the fission trigger explodes with an explosive yield of a few tens of kilotons, the first fusion stage would explode with a yield of several hundred kilotons, and the second fusion stage, if present, would yield several megatons. For example, the Soviet Union exploded an H-bomb in 1962 with a yield equal to that of 58 million tons of TNT – equivalent to about 3,000 Nagasaki bombs. This was probably a three-stage device, with a fission trigger which exploded with a power of several hundred kilotons, and two fusion stages. Even higher yields could be obtained.

Improving warhead accuracies

The target assigned to a nuclear warhead is determined by the combination of its explosive yield and the accuracy with which it can be delivered. Recent technological advances have considerably increased the accuracy of the delivery of nuclear warheads. Modern American nuclear weapons illustrate the accuracies now possible.

The accuracy of a nuclear warhead is normally measured by its circular error probability, or CEP, defined as the radius of the circle centred on the target within which a half of a large number of warheads of the same type fired at the target will fall. The Americans have continually improved the guidance system of their intercontinental ballistic missiles so that the CEP has been considerably reduced. For example, the CEP of a Minuteman II warhead, first deployed in 1966, is about 370 metres; the new American intercontinental ballistic missile – the MX – has a CEP of about 100 metres. The latest Russian intercontinental ballistic missile, the SS-25 Sickle, has a CEP of about 200 metres (International Institute for Strategic Studies 1991).

Similar developments are taking place in submarine-launched ballistic missiles. The new American Trident D-5 submarine-launched ballistic missile, for example, has a CEP of about 120 metres whereas the CEP of the older Trident C-4 is 450 metres. Warheads with CEPs of about 100 metres or less are war-fighting weapons.

Trident-2 and MX warheads may eventually be fitted with terminal guidance, in which a laser or radar set in the nose of the warhead scans the ground around the target as the warhead travels towards it through the earth's atmosphere. The laser or radar locks on to a distinctive feature in the area, such as a tall building or hill, and guides the warhead with great accuracy on to its target. With terminal guidance, Trident-2 and MX warheads will have CEPs of 40 metres or so.

Nuclear policies

Now that the Cold War is over, the Iron Curtain has gone, Germany is reunited, and the Soviet military threat has evaporated, what nuclear policies are being evolved to suit the new international order? The evolution of these policies may be determined more by the technological advances incorporated into nuclear weapons than by foreign-policy considerations.

Over the years, the nuclear arms race has acquired a technological momentum which has caused, and is causing, changes in Russian and American nuclear strategies. It seems likely that the authorities in Moscow will continue to control the former Soviet nuclear forces and determine nuclear strategies.

The formation of large teams of nuclear scientists and technologists to operate military nuclear reactors and other nuclear-weapon facilities, and to design, develop, test and produce nuclear weapons eventually results in the emergence of powerful lobbies of professionals, who want to design and produce increasingly sophisticated nuclear weapons just to convince themselves that they can do so and for the satisfaction of it.

These lobbies become part of the political process, which together with the other elements of the defence establishment generate inputs into the decision-making process, in favour of the continual modernization of nuclear weapons and their supporting technologies; inputs so strong as to be very difficult for political leaders to overcome. Nuclear strategies are then mainly determined not by the requirements of rational foreign-policy considerations but by the technological characteristics of nuclear weapons and their supporting technologies. (This argument applies to the small nuclear powers – including, for example, Israel – as well as to the two big ones.)

The American administration has made it clear that it intends to continue to modernize its nuclear weapons and their supporting technologies, even though there is no obvious enemy at which to aim a sophisticated nuclear force. Research and development in anti-submarine warfare and anti-ballistic missile systems will continue. These developments will have consequences for nuclear policies.

Nuclear deterrence by assured destruction

The targets at which nuclear weapons are aimed, no matter which country owns them, are generally determined by the accuracy with which the weapons can be delivered. Inaccurate nuclear weapons are seen to be useful for nuclear deterrence, by threatening an enemy with unacceptable death and destruction; accurate nuclear weapons are seen as more useful for fighting a nuclear war than for deterring one by assured destruction.

The policy of nuclear deterrence by assured destruction rests on four tenets. First, the nuclear forces of the deterrer must be fashioned exclusively for retaliation in response to an attack by the other side's weapons of mass destruction or in response to a threat of annihilation. Second, the nuclear forces – including their command and control systems – must be capable of prompt action. Third, the threat on which the deterrence rests must be the killing of a large fraction of the enemy population and the destruction of much of its economy. Fourth, the enemy must be aware of the threat in time to deter it from making the actions that will provoke the massive retaliation.

The commonly held view that the very destructiveness of nuclear weapons precludes the outbreak of nuclear war is false. Even if 'rational' behaviour is assumed, nuclear war is unlikely to occur only if it is believed that neither side can win. If one power perceives a chance of winning, then there is a risk that it will decide to strike while it has the advantage. Moreover, in a serious crisis, the side which perceives that it is at a disadvantage may, if it believes that the use of weapons of mass destruction is very likely, attack first, and perhaps prematurely, in the hope of reducing the damage it thinks it is almost bound to suffer.

A relatively small number of nuclear weapons are needed for assured destruction. All that is needed is the number of nuclear weapons required to target the enemy's significant cities. Even in both the USA and the Commonwealth of Independent States, for example, there are at most 200 cities with populations greater than about 100,000 people. If the relations between states, even hostile ones, are being determined rationally, a very small number of nuclear weapons which can be reliably delivered on to their targets are enough for a minimum nuclear deterrent. For the USA and the former Soviet Union, this number is certainly much less than a hundred.

A paradox of the nuclear age is that nuclear deterrence based on mutual assured destruction (MAD), if it works at all, only does so with inaccurate nuclear weapons. As more accurate nuclear weapons are deployed the enemy may assume that your nuclear weapons are targeted on his nuclear forces and not on his cities. The cities then cease to be effective hostages. In other words, accurate nuclear weapons weaken and eventually kill nuclear deterrence based on assured destruction.

With nuclear weapons accurate enough to destroy even very hardened military targets, nuclear war-fighting based on the destruction of hostile military forces becomes the preferred policy. Accurate nuclear weapons change nuclear strategy from nuclear deterrence to nuclear war-fighting, whether or not the political leadership wants to make the change.

Unless military nuclear technology is brought under control, a nuclear war-fighting strategy will give way to a nuclear war-winning one, which is seen to give a nuclear strategic superiority. A range of military technologies is being developed that will strengthen military and political perceptions about the possibility of fighting and winning a nuclear war. The most important of these technologies are those related to anti-submarine warfare and anti-ballistic missile systems.

If one side could severely limit the damage that the other side's strategic nuclear submarines could create in a retaliatory strike, and it believed it could destroy, by anti-ballistic missiles, the enemy missile warheads which survived a surprise attack, then the temptation to make an all-out first strike might become strong.

Developments in anti-submarine warfare are particularly disturbing. Now that land-based ballistic missiles are vulnerable to a first (pre-emptive) nuclear strike by hostile land-based missiles, nuclear deterrence depends mainly on the continuing invulnerability of nuclear strategic submarines. If strategic nuclear submarines do become vulnerable, a first nuclear strike may be seen as desirable and even essential to prevent the other side from itself acquiring a first-strike capability. Moreover, moves to nuclear war-fighting and war-winning strategies considerably increase the risk of nuclear war by accident.

All the declared nuclear-weapon powers are improving the quality of the nuclear weapons – an activity usually referred to as 'modernization'. And Israel seems to be following the same path. Political leaders seem unable to control the momentum of nuclear-weapon technology. New nuclear policies are adopted to justify the deployment of new nuclear weapons.

Nuclear war-fighting and war-winning

The move from nuclear deterrence by mutual assured destruction (MAD) to nuclear war-fighting is virtually certain if large numbers of accurate nuclear weapons are deployed. These are, in military jargon, 'counter-force' rather than 'counter-city'. A nuclear war-fighting policy can justify the deployment of a large number of nuclear weapons.

'War-fighting deterrence', as the present policy has been called, will give way to war-winning strategies, in which it is argued that victory is possible in a nuclear war. A range of military technologies is being developed that will strengthen military and political perceptions about the possibility of fighting and winning a nuclear war. The most important of these technologies are those related to anti-submarine warfare

(ASW), anti-ballistic missile (ABM) systems, and anti-satellite warfare systems.

If one side could severely limit the damage that the other side's strategic nuclear submarines could create in a retaliatory strike, and it believed it could destroy, by anti-ballistic missiles, the enemy missile warheads which survived a surprise attack, then the temptation to make an all-out first strike might become virtually irresistible, particularly during a period of international crisis. Hence the importance of developments in ASW and in ABM systems.

ASW systems

Now that land-based ballistic missiles are vulnerable to a first (pre-emptive) nuclear strike by hostile land-based missiles, east–west nuclear deterrence depends mainly on the continuing invulnerability of strategic nuclear submarines. If strategic nuclear submarines become vulnerable, a first nuclear strike may be seen as desirable and even essential to prevent the enemy from himself acquiring a first-strike capability.

ASW systems are designed to detect, identify and destroy enemy submarines. Modern submarines are very effective if they get within range of enemy warships. The best way of dealing with them is to engage them before they get within range.

To attack enemy submarines at long range, the American navy, for example, relies mainly on long-range maritime patrol aircraft, particularly the P-3 Orion, and on its own attack submarines. The Long Range ASW Aircraft (LRAACA), a land-based four-engine ASW patrol aircraft, a derivative of the P-3 design, is under development to supplement the P-3.

Any enemy submarines that evade detection at long range will be attacked by the surface warships. An American carrier battle group, for example, will use formations of surface ships carrying passive and active sonar systems to detect hostile submarines and torpedo-armed helicopters to attack them.

In ASW, detection is the critical element. Detection methods are being improved by increasing the sensitivity of detectors, improving the integration between various sensing systems, and improving the computer processing of the data collected by sensors.

The main categories of ASW sensors are electronic, based on radar, infra-red or lasers; optical; acoustic, particularly active and passive sonar; and magnetic, particularly the Magnetic Anomaly Detector (MAD), in which the disturbance to the earth's magnetic field caused by the presence of the submarine is measured. Sensors may be carried on aircraft and ships, deployed on satellites in space, or fixed to the bottom of the ocean.

Sonar devices rely on sound to detect objects in the ocean. Although light doesn't travel well through water, sound does. During the Second World War, the development of underwater acoustic technology accelerated rapidly, spurred on by the needs of anti-submarine warfare. The technology led to the development of Sound Navigation And Ranging – or sonar.

In an active sonar device, a pulse of sound is transmitted from the sonar transmitter. If, in its passage through the ocean, it hits an object like a submarine, some of the sound will be reflected back and some of the 'echo' will be collected by the sonar receiver. The time taken for the sound to travel to the object – a submarine, for example – and back to the sonar receiver is measured. From this time and the known velocity of sound, the distance to the submarine is calculated. If a number of sonars are used, the directions the echoes come from give the position of the submarine. A typical sonar system, which may, for example, be towed behind a ship, is an array of acoustic transducers. A transducer acts as both a transmitter and a receiver, emitting short pulses (bursts) of sound waves at regular intervals and listening for echoes between the pulses.

The ASW activities of the USA are global and continuous, involving a total system of great technological complexity, including the use of a network of foreign bases. In American ASW activities, fixed undersea surveillance systems, based on arrays of hydrophones and monitoring a large area of ocean, play a key role. (A hydrophone is an electro-acoustic transducer used to detect sounds transmitted through water.) Mobile and air-dropped systems supplement the fixed sea-bottom sensors.

The US navy operates special ships, called Tagos Ocean Surveillance Ships, which are platforms for the Surveillance Tower-Array Sensor System (SURTASS), with long-range surveillance capabilities to extend ASW coverage to those parts of the world's oceans not covered by the fixed ocean-bottom systems. P-3 Orion aircraft, which operate from a number of bases throughout the world, are provided with information about the general location of Russian submarines. The aircraft then use large numbers of sonobuoys, and sophisticated computers to process the data and pinpoint the submarines. A sonobuoy is dropped and floats on the sea to pick up noise from any submarine and transmit a bearing of it to the aircraft. Three such bearings enable the aircraft to fix the position of the submarine.

ASW systems are also carried on surface warships, particularly cruisers and destroyers. American warships, for example, carry the Tactical Towed Array Sonar (TACTAS) system in which a network of sonobuoys is towed behind a ship to detect any submarine in the vicinity. ASW helicopters are carried on the ships and used to attack any submarines detected with torpedoes or depth charges. An example of such a helicopter is the American SH-60B Seahawk Light Airborne Multipurpose System (LAMPS) Mk III, a computer-integrated ship helicopter system which deploys sonobuoys and processes information from them. It is also a platform for radar and electronic warfare support measures. The SH-60F is a derivation of the SH-60B, providing quick-reaction inner-zone protection for a carrier battle group using an improved tethered sonar.

The most effective weapon system for detecting and attacking enemy submarines is another submarine – the hunter-killer submarine. A hunter-killer is usually a nuclear-powered submarine equipped with ASW sensors, underwater communications equipment, computers for data analysis, and computers to fire and control ASW weapons, particularly torpedoes and ASW missiles. Once detected, enemy submarines can be destroyed with torpedoes, missiles or depth charges. The Americans are now developing two new long-range ASW missiles that will be able to attack enemy submarines at distances beyond torpedo range.

ABM systems

The Pentagon is planning the Phase One Strategic Defense System as the initial deployment of an ABM system. It argues that Phase One – known as Global Protection Against Limited Strikes (GPALS) – is technically achievable and could be deployed by the year 2000. It is a layered defensive system consisting of ground- and space-based interceptors, their support systems and a command centre.

There is now no pretence that an ABM system could protect the whole of the USA against a full-scale Russian strategic attack. The rationale for GPALS is to defend against an accidental attack involving one or a small number of missiles, a limited attack launched by a mad military commander, and a future attack by a Third World country involving a few long-range missiles. The system is supposed to defend against a ballistic-missile attack of up to 200 nuclear warheads.

In the space-based layer, Brilliant Pebbles missiles, now under development, are designed to destroy enemy ICBMs in their boost phase, before they release their warheads and decoys. The ground-based interceptor missile, the High-altitude Endoatmospheric Defense Interceptor (HEDI), will attack enemy warheads which survive the Brilliant Pebbles shortly after they re-enter the earth's atmosphere. HEDI is in an advanced stage of development.

The Boost Surveillance and Tracking System (BSTS) will detect enemy missile-launches, acquire and track the boosters, and assess the number of missiles destroyed. The Space Surveillance and Tracking System (SSTS) will acquire and track post-boost vehicles and re-entry vehicles, satellites and anti-satellite weapons, and assess the destruction of enemy warheads. The Airborne Optical Adjunct (AOA), an infra-red radiation sensor system carried on a Boeing-767 aircraft to track warheads in their mid-course and terminal stages, is in an advanced stage of development.

The Ground-based Surveillance and Tracking System (GSTS) will discriminate between re-entry warheads and decoys, track re-entry vehicles and decoys, and assess the destruction of enemy warheads. GSTS will probably be complemented by a railway-deployed Ground-Based Radar (GBR) system. The command centre will link all these systems and control the space battle.

Each Brilliant Pebble is a self-contained system, consisting of a light-weight missile including integrated sensors, guidance and control. Current plans for GPALS involve the deployment of Brilliant Pebbles, encased in protective bullet-shaped cases, on a thousand or so satellites orbiting at altitudes of about 960 kilometres. Each missile is about 1 metre long, 0.3 metres wide, and weighs about 45 kilograms; each will be provided with a solar cell to keep its systems charged. In addition, the deployment of between 750 and 1,000 HEDI anti-ballistic missiles is called for.

When the satellites are commanded, by coded signal, to release the Brilliant Pebbles, the protective cases open and the missiles are released. Each Brilliant Pebble carries sensors to detect ultra-violet and infra-red radiation. These can pick up the radiations from the exhaust flames of the rockets of enemy ballistic missiles as they are launched from their silos. The Brilliant Pebble's computer would then calculate the speed and trajectory of the enemy missile and programme itself on to an interception course. The Pebble's rocket motor would fire and direct it on a collision course with the missile. The Pebble would depend on the kinetic energy of impact to destroy its target missile.

If the current thaw in international relations continues, funding applications for GPALS, including Brilliant Pebbles, will have a rough ride in the US Congress. But research and development of more advanced Star Wars concepts, including high-powered free-electron and chemical lasers and neutral particle beam weapons, continues in the hope of a deployment option in several years' time.

The perceived success of the US Patriot surface-to-air missile against Iraqi SCUD surface-to-surface missile attacks against Israel and Saudi Arabia gave a considerable boost to theatre anti-ballistic missiles to defend against attacks by tactical ballistic missiles. The plan is to deploy anti-tactical ballistic missiles with American forces stationed around the world. Current American research and development programmes include improvements for the Patriot system; the Extended Range Interceptor (ERINT); the Arrow missile, a joint American–Israeli programme to develop a high-altitude interceptor; and the Theater High Altitude Area Defence (THAAD) system.

6

THE SPREAD OF NUCLEAR WEAPONS

The proliferation of nuclear weapons to countries that do not now have them is a crucial international issue. Currently, there are five established nuclear-weapon powers: the USA, Russia, the UK, France and China. These powers regularly test nuclear weapons, and we have significant information about the numbers, types and technical characteristics of their nuclear arsenals. Israel is known to have nuclear weapons, although the Israeli government has consistently refused to confirm this.

The total number of nuclear weapons in the world's arsenals is about 50,000. The ex-Soviet arsenal has about 27,000; the USA has about 20,000; France has about 600; the UK has about 400; China has about 250; and Israel has about 150 (Norris *et al*. 1991). A number of other countries are on the threshold of becoming nuclear-weapon powers.

India tested a nuclear device in 1974, demonstrating its capability to produce a nuclear force, but the Indian government claims that it has no stockpile of nuclear weapons. Pakistan is generally believed to be on the threshold of producing nuclear weapons and may have already done so. Argentina and Brazil are believed capable of producing nuclear weapons, but both countries have apparently moved away from a political decision to do so.

Other Third World countries who could, if they take the political decision to do so, produce nuclear weapons in a relatively short time include Taiwan, South Korea and possibly North Korea. Iraq was suspected of developing nuclear weapons before the Gulf War, and Iran is also suspected of having ambitions to produce a nuclear force.

Peaceful versus military atoms

Any country with a peaceful nuclear-power programme has the plutonium and the expertise to produce nuclear weapons. The peaceful atom and the military atom are intimately linked – 'Siamese twins', in the words of one Nobel Prizewinning nuclear physicist. The spread of nuclear-power reactors is, therefore, of fundamental importance to any consideration of the spread of nuclear weapons.

Between President Eisenhower's Atoms for Peace programme in the mid-1950s and the early 1980s the nuclear industry expanded rapidly. The oil-price increase in 1973 was a particular boost for it. A number of important countries like France and Japan became intent on reducing their dependence on oil imports by installing nuclear-power reactors. Another boost was the concern over the contribution to the greenhouse effect, and hence to global warming, from the atmospheric pollution produced by the burning of fossil fuels in power stations. Nuclear electricity was promoted as being environmentally friendly.

During the 1980s, however, the nuclear-power industry suffered a series of setbacks. The first was the realization that nuclear electricity was relatively very expensive. And in 1986 came the Chernobyl nuclear accident. Reactor safety became a second major challenge to the nuclear-power industry. The difficulty of finding a poltically and publicly acceptable solution to the problem of the disposal of high-level radioactive waste and concern about the health effects of low-level radiation added to doubts about nuclear power.

In 1970, the world's nuclear-power reactors were generating a total of about 20 giga-watts of electricity (1 giga-watt of electricity, or GWe, is 1,000 million watts of electricity). Five years later, this total had about quadrupled, to 75 GWe in 1975. It took another fifteen years for the total to quadruple again. Today, the total world's nuclear generating capacity is 326 GWe, generated by 423 power reactors in twenty-five countries – the USA, France, the Commonwealth of Independent States, Japan, Germany, Canada, the UK, Sweden, South Korea, and Spain (IAEA 1991). These top ten account for 91 per cent of the total. The other countries operating nuclear-power reactors are Argentina, Belgium, Brazil, Bulgaria, Czechoslovakia, Finland, Hungary, India, Mexico, the Netherlands, Pakistan, South Africa, Switzerland, Taiwan and Yugoslavia. Four other countries – China, Cuba, Iran and Romania – which now have no nuclear power are constructing power reactors.

In the year 2000 the world's nuclear generating capacity will be about 400 GWe. There are at present eighty-three nuclear-power reactors under construction. When completed, these will add 66 GWe to the world's nuclear capacity.

Plutonium production

As the uranium fuel elements in a power reactor are burned to produce heat from the fission process (which is used to produce steam from boiling water to run turbines to generate electricity) fission products and plutonium are produced. Spent reactor fuel elements are so radio-active, because of the fission products in them, that they are self-protecting. But if the plutonium is removed from the fuel elements and separated from the fission products, in a chemical reprocessing plant, it is in a form that can be relatively easily handled. As the amount of plutonium produced worldwide in civilian nuclear-power reactors and separated from spent reactor fuel elements in commercial reprocessing plants increases it will become easier for governments (and sub-national groups) to obtain it illegally. Whether or not to reprocess is, therefore, a crucial political decision.

The world's civilian nuclear-power reactors have so far produced about 700 tonnes of plutonium, and are producing about 75 tonnes a year. By the year 2000, the world's civilian reactors will have produced a total of about 1,700 tonnes of plutonium and will be producing some 100 tonnes a year (Albright and Feiveson 1991).

About 90 tonnes of civilian plutonium have so far been chemically separated from spent reactor fuel elements in reprocessing plants out-side the Commonwealth of Independent States. By 2000, according to current plans, some 300 tonnes will have been separated. For compari-son, the amount of military plutonium in the world's nuclear arsenal is about 220 tons. By 2000, large commercial reprocessing plants will be operating in the UK, France, Russia and Japan.

Plutonium is produced as an inevitable by-product in all nuclear reactors. But the isotopic composition of the plutonium produced in reactors operated for different purposes varies. The plutonium pro-duced specifically for military purposes is rich in the isotope plu-tonium-239. 'Weapons-grade' plutonium typically contains more than 93 per cent of the isotope plutonium-239 and is the material which produces the most efficient nuclear weapons. Plutonium produced in nuclear-power reactors operated to produce electricity in the most economical way, known as reactor-grade, typically contains only about 60 per cent plutonium-239. About 25 per cent is plutonium-240 (in weapons-grade plutonium the amount is typically about 7 per cent) and about 10 per cent is plutonium-241.

Can this reactor-grade plutonium be used to produce nuclear explosions? This is an important question because, if it can, countries operating nuclear-power reactors for peaceful purposes, particularly electricity production, have access to plutonium that could be used to produce nuclear weapons. And, as the quantity of reactor-grade plutonium in the world increases, it becomes easier for a country to acquire it illegally – on a plutonium black market, for example – and produce nuclear weapons. That reactor-grade plutonium can be used to produce a nuclear weapon has been shown in the USA, where at least two such devices have been built and tested.

51

The critical mass of typical reactor-grade plutonium in the form of a bare metal sphere surrounded by a natural uranium reflector, about 10 centimetres thick, is about 7 kilograms. Reactor-grade plutonium is usually stored, after reprocessing, in the form of plutonium oxide and is, therefore, most likely to be available in this form. The oxide can, however, be easily converted to the metal form.

The removal of plutonium from reactor fuel elements is a relatively straightforward chemical process. If operated commercially, for a profit, a plutonium-reprocessing plant is a complex and costly chemical establishment and, because the capital cost is relatively independent of the size of the plant, economic reprocessing can only be achieved if a large-scale plant is used to serve many reactors. A typical modern commercial reprocessing plant will reprocess about 1,200 tons of spent reactor fuel a year, containing about 12 tons of plutonium, and service about forty modern nuclear-power reactors.

Clandestine production of fissile material

To obtain plutonium for military purposes, where money is no object, reprocessing can easily be done on a small scale. In fact, a country could obtain plutonium clandestinely from a nuclear reactor acquired especially for the purpose. The components for a small reactor, capable of producing enough plutonium to make a few nuclear weapons a year, can be easily, and secretly, obtained on the open market for roughly $30 million (about the same cost as a modern fighter aircraft).

The reactor and a small reprocessing facility to remove the plutonium from the reactor fuel elements could be clandestinely constructed and operated. These units, and room to design and construct nuclear weapons from the plutonium, could be effectively disguised and hidden in a building or underground. Israel used a clandestine reactor and reprocessing facility to produce plutonium for its nuclear force.

Some countries choose enriched uranium rather than plutonium as the fissile material for nuclear weapons. Three methods are available for enriching uranium: the gas diffusion, the gas centrifuge and the jet nozzle techniques. The technique mainly used so far is the gas diffusion method. But, given the materials now available, particularly carbon fibre, countries wishing to enrich uranium would probably opt for the gas centrifuge method. Pakistan is using this route to produce fissile material for nuclear weapons, and Iraq was in the process of doing so before the Gulf War.

A gas centrifuge for uranium enrichment consists of a vacuum tank containing a long rotating drum with a nozzle at one end and an orifice at the other. Uranium hexafluoride gas is pumped in via the nozzle and, as the gas moves up inside the rotating drum, molecules of the uranium hexafluoride gas will tend to be flung outwards by the centrifugal force. Molecules of uranium hexafluoride gas in which the uranium is uranium-238 are slightly heavier than molecules of uranium-235 hexafluoride. There will, therefore, be a difference in the centrifugal force acting on the molecules of different masses when the gas is rotated at very high speed. Molecules of the lighter uranium-235 isotope will diffuse towards the centre. The inner portion thus becomes enriched in uranium-235, and this is collected at the exit orifice.

A plant containing many gas centrifuges in a cascade is needed to enrich a useful quantity of uranium. The slightly enriched flow of uranium gas from the first centrifuge is fed into the nozzle of the next centrifuge in the cascade and so on. The uranium is circulated around the cascade until the desired degree of enrichment is obtained. A gas-centrifuge plant for a nuclear-weapon programme could, like a military plutonium facility, be constructed clandestinely.

Because the basic design of nuclear weapons using nuclear fission is now well known and the nuclear data needed are in the open literature, and because the facilities to produce plutonium and enriched uranium for nuclear weapons can be built and operated secretly and simply, we do not know for sure which countries have nuclear weapons bombs and which do not. A nuclear-weapon programme could be kept secret until a nuclear test was performed.

The need for nuclear testing

A nuclear test removes all ambiguity about a country's nuclear-weapon programme. This is, of course, why any country wishing to hide nuclear-weapon developments would want to avoid testing.

An important question is whether or not the military and political leaders would be prepared to accept nuclear weapons unless and until the designs have been tested with full-scale nuclear tests. In particular, the military may require to know the precise explosive power of any weapons under its control and may demand tests to check that estimated yields can, in practice, be achieved within relatively narrow limits.

So far as today's nuclear-weapon designers are concerned, they will probably be so confident that they could design and construct ordinary nuclear weapons using implosion (i.e., a Nagasaki-type design) that they would not need a full-scale test – at least, when weapons-grade fissile material is used. Nor would testing be requested if enriched uranium is used in a gun-type design. Testing is, however, likely to be called for if reactor-grade plutonium were used.

The designers would probably be sure that the weapons would produce explosive yields within their predicted range. Provided that the fissile material used was weapons-grade uranium or plutonium, the designers could predict the explosive power rather precisely, within a narrow range. Also, the scientists and engineers who built the weapons would be confident that they would explode according to the design.

Whether or not the military will take the word of the nuclear scientists and engineers that the nuclear weapons they design and build will work reliably according to their predictions will depend on the attitude of the military to science and technology. If a significant fraction of the senior military officers are technically minded, it is likely that the military will accept the word of the scientists.

But nuclear weapons that include an element of nuclear fusion are a different matter. The designers of boosted nuclear weapons and of full-scale thermonuclear weapons will want to test them. Even today, the design of a thermonuclear weapon is a very complex matter.

The test of a thermonuclear weapon need not involve testing the entire assembly at full explosive power. It would normally be enough to test the fission trigger plus a small section of the fusion component to test that the fusion process was set off. The yield of the test may be relatively low. If the scaled-down device produces some fusion, it can be assumed that the full-scale weapon will work effectively.

To hide a nuclear explosion with an explosive power greater than, say, 10 kt is a difficult task, even if it is set off deep below ground. Such an explosion can normally be detected by seismic monitoring equipment operated outside the country in which the nuclear explosion takes place. The Indian explosion in May 1974 of a 12 kt nuclear device was, for example, easily detected. And the Indian explosion, set off at a depth of about 100 metres underground in the Rajasthan desert, produced a crater in the ground of 150 metres in diameter which was easily observed by reconnaissance satellites.

The key components of a nuclear weapon could be tested without a full-scale nuclear test. Pakistan is said to have done so. The design of a fission weapon could be tested by, for example, using only a small sphere of fissile material at the centre of the conventional chemical explosive lens system. The sphere could be sufficiently small that, when the core is exploded, the nuclear fission yield produces an explosion of a power about the same as that of the conventional explosive (i.e., 200 kilograms or less). This amount of fission would be sufficient to be detected by radiation detectors placed around the test assembly.

The detection of a burst of radiation, particularly neutrons, would show that an effective implosion has taken place. But the explosion would be insufficiently powerful to be detected by seismic monitors outside the country concerned.

7

NUCLEAR TERRORISM

Trends in the relations between states involve increasing risks that weapons of mass destruction, nuclear, chemical and biological, will be acquired by groups other than legal governments. The break-up of the former Soviet Union into a number of nation states, for example, carries with it the risk that some of the 27,000 or so nuclear weapons, now under firm political and military control, will fall into the hands of people who do not have, and do not want, access to the normal command and control structures.

The ex-Soviet arsenal also contains large numbers of chemical weapons. These are deployed in munition stores located in many places across the former Soviet Union. Nuclear and chemical weapons may, in short, be stolen, sold or transferred to other countries or groups.

Established subnational groups – commonly, and usually disparagingly, referred to by the catch-all term 'terrorists' – may well decide to move to higher levels of killing. It would be surprising if the leaders of sub-national groups have not yet thought about using weapons of mass destruction, based on nuclear, chemical or biological systems. Presumably, they have until now decided that killing, or threatening to kill, large numbers of people indiscriminantly, and/or contaminating large areas, would not further their ends.

But this attitude may well change. As time goes on, terrorists are becoming more sophisticated and skilled. At the same time, wars, and society itself, are becoming more violent. We must expect that moral restraints on mass killing will weaken.

The frequent use of chemical weapons, including nerve gases, in the Iran–Iraq War and the use by Iraq of nerve gas against its Kurdish citizens, and the lack of strong international condemnation of these uses indicate that this is, in fact, already happening.

The recent sabotage of Air India and PanAm jumbo jets shows a trend to increasing terrorist violence. A future rung on the terrorists' ladder of escalation may well be the use of nuclear, chemical or biological weapons.

Peter Calvocoressi points out:

> Various types of belligerence fit uneasily into an international
> state system. With the growth of power of the state it has become
> common to label as war only those kinds of organized violence
> which are conducted by a state . . . but there remain further
> kinds of belligerence, commonly disparaged as terrorism. This is
> a word to beware of. It has become a term of abuse used to
> excite prejudice and fuel unthinking reactions – which is all the
> more deplorable since terrorism does exist and has to be
> countered.
>
> (Calvocoressi 1987)

Calvocoressi's warning is particularly apt when dealing with the possibility that weapons of mass destruction will spread outside the control of sovereign states.

Terrorism is defined as criminal violence by minorities using 'coercive terror' for political ends. Terrorism – i.e., sub-national violence for political reasons – can succeed in its purpose in politics, and violence can be made to pay. This lesson was, in fact, dramatically demonstrated in the Middle East when, after the Second World War, Jewish 'terrorists' in Palestine, including the Irgun and Stern organizations, played a – if not *the* – major role in driving out the British and establishing in 1948 the State of Israel.

Perhaps because of its successes, or perceived successes, terrorism is on the increase. That this is happening when access to materials, equipment and technologies useful for the acquisition of nuclear, chemical and biological weapons is becoming easier is a cause of considerable concern.

The theft of plutonium

Nuclear terrorism is thought by most people to be a more terrifying prospect than chemical or biological terrorism. For reasons that are not very clear, the nuclear threat is more credible and effective than the chemical or biological one.

Until recently, the majority of commentators argued that the most likely way in which a sub-national group would acquire a nuclear explosive was by stealing a nuclear weapon from a nuclear-weapon stockpile or hijacking a nuclear warhead when it was being transported. But, as plutonium becomes more available, it is increasingly likely that a sub-national group will steal, or otherwise illegally acquire, plutonium and construct its own nuclear explosive device to detonate it or threaten to detonate it.

Although this may be the most likely form of nuclear terrorism, there are other possibilities. Konrad Kellen lists them as 'the damaging of a nuclear plant for radioactive release; the attack on a nuclear-weapons site to spread alarm; the attack on a nuclear plant to spread alarm; the holding of a nuclear plant for blackmail; the holding off-site of nuclear plant personnel; the theft of fissionable material for blackmail or radioactive release; the theft or sabotage of things nuclear for demonstration purposes; and an attack on a transporter of nuclear weapons or materials' (Kellen 1987).

We will concentrate here on the main risk – that a sub-national group will in the future illegally acquire fissile material and itself construct a nuclear explosive. Although a sub-national group could choose to use either plutonium or highly enriched uranium as the fissionable material for nuclear explosives, plutonium is increasingly the more likely option. Currently, roughly 17,000 kilograms of highly enriched uranium are used throughout the world, mainly to fuel about 140 civilian research reactors in some fifty countries. But the development of new low-enriched uranium fuels for use in research reactors will sharply reduce the amount of highly enriched uranium in circulation. The amount of plutonium available, however, will rapidly increase.

Other factors which increase the risk of nuclear terrorism include the relatively small amount of plutonium needed to fabricate a nuclear explosive, the availability in the open literature of the technical information needed to fabricate a nuclear device, and the small number of competent people needed to fabricate a primitive nuclear device.

As the amount of plutonium produced worldwide in civilian nuclear-power reactors and separated from spent reactor fuel elements in commercial reprocessing plants increases it will become easier to obtain plutonium illegally. As we have seen, about 90 tonnes of civilian plutonium have so far been chemically separated from spent reactor fuel elements in reprocessing plants outside the Commonwealth of Independent States. By 2000, according to current plans, some 300 tonnes will have been separated by large commercial reprocessing plants operating in the UK, France and Japan.

Even with the best available or foreseeable safeguards technology, it is virtually impossible to detect the diversion (i.e., theft) of an amount of plutonium sufficient to produce a nuclear explosive when thousands of kilograms are separated a year (safeguards on reprocessing plants are unlikely to be better than 1 or 2 per cent effective). This is why the current concern is that sub-national groups (including terrorists, liberation movements and criminals) will get their hands on plutonium, let alone that governments will do so for the production of nuclear weapons.

Apart from its use as an explosive, plutonium can be used as a fuel for fast-breeder reactors (in which, by a cunning design, more plutonium is produced than is burned as fuel) and as a fuel for ordinary (thermal) power reactors. For use in thermal reactors, plutonium oxide is mixed with natural uranium oxide to produce a mixed-oxide (MOX) blend which is then made into fuel elements for use in, for example, pressurized-water reactors.

MOX would be vulnerable to theft by terrorist or other sub-national groups as it is transported from the fuel-fabrication plant to the various reactors which will use it as fuel. In fact, the theft of plutonium in MOX fuel elements is probably the most likely way in which such groups will, in the future, obtain plutonium.

Plutonium will, in any case, be increasingly transported worldwide on virtually all the main transport systems – road, rail, sea and air – and, therefore, be increasingly vulnerable to theft. This transport will occur because plutonium commercially reprocessed in countries outside the Commonwealth of Independent States, particularly France and the UK, is normally returned to its owners.

The spent fuel elements from nuclear-power reactors exported by the former Soviet Union to other ex-communist countries have been taken back and stored. If the elements are reprocessed, the plutonium has been kept by the Soviets and not returned to the country that owns it. Plutonium produced in Soviet power reactors or Soviet-supplied reactors has, up to now, been relatively secure from theft.

The disintegration of the Soviet Union and the instability of eastern Europe may, however, make the theft of plutonium produced in Soviet-supplied reactors more likely. There is a very serious danger that no authority in these countries will protect fissile material properly and that doing so will have a low priority, given the seriousness of all their other problems.

Reactor-grade plutonium as an explosive

After reprocessing, reactor-grade plutonium is normally stored as plutonium oxide rather than as plutonium metal. The critical mass of reactor-grade plutonium in the form of plutonium-oxide crystals is about 35 kilograms, if in spherical shape. The radius of this sphere of plutonium oxide would be about 9 centimetres. Reactor-grade plutonium oxide in uncompacted powder form has a critical mass of about 875 kilograms if in a sphere; the radius of the sphere would be about 45 centimetres.

If a sub-national group acquires plutonium oxide, it may convert it to plutonium metal, which can be done using straightforward chemical methods. The critical mass of reactor-grade plutonium in metal form is about 15 kilograms.

The main problem with using reactor-grade plutonium as a nuclear weapon is that the spontaneous fission rate of plutonium-240 is much greater than that of plutonium-239. In reactor-grade plutonium the average time between spontaneous fissions is less than a micro-second (a millionth of a second). This means that very fast implosion techniques would be necessary in a nuclear device made from reactor-grade plutonium to prevent pre-detonation, which leads to uncertain explosive yields.

Spontaneous fission produces a neutron background in a weapon-grade plutonium core of about one neutron every two or three micro-seconds. With a mean time of a few micro-seconds between neutrons – a very much longer time than the duration of the fission chain reaction – radial compression rates of a few millimetres per micro-second will prevent pre-detonation. Implosion techniques can achieve this without much difficulty.

But for reactor-grade plutonium the mean time between neutrons is a small fraction of a micro-second. Extremely fast assembly would be needed to achieve super-criticality. Implosions technologies to provide the very high shock velocities and compression needed to prevent pre-detonation are available but probably not to a sub-national group – at least, in the foreseeable future.

Is it easy to make a nuclear explosive?

The ease with which a sub-national group could construct a nuclear weapon is discussed in detail by Mark et al. (Mark et al. 1987). Because this group of authors includes experienced nuclear-weapon designers it is worth giving their conclusions in some detail. They say that, so far as crude nuclear devices (devices guaranteed to work without the need for extensive theoretical or experimental demonstration) are concerned:

1 Such a device could be constructed by a group not previously engaged in designing or building nuclear weapons, providing a number of requirements are adequately met.
2 Successful execution would require the efforts of a team having knowledge and skills additional to those usually associated with a group engaged in hijacking a transport or conducting a raid on a plant.
3 To achieve rapid turnaround (that is, to make the device ready within a day or so of obtaining the material), careful preparations extending over a considerable period would have to be carried out, and the materials acquired would have to be in the form prepared for.

4 The amounts of fissile material necessary would tend to be large – certainly several times the minimum quantity required by expert and experienced nuclear-weapon designers.

5 The weight of the complete device would also be large – not as large as the first atomic weapons (about 4.5 tons), since these required aerodynamic cases to enable them to be handled as bombs, but probably more than a ton.

6 The conceivable option of using oxide powder (whether of uranium or plutonium) directly, with no post-acquisition processing or fabrication, would seem to be the simplest and most rapid way to make a bomb. However, the amount of material required would be considerably greater than if metal were used.

7 There are a number of obvious potential hazards in any such operation, among them those arising in the handling of a high explosive; the possibility of inadvertently inducing a critical configuration of the fissile material at some stage in the procedure; and the chemical toxicity or radiological hazards inherent in the materials used. Failure to foresee all the needs on these points could bring the operation to a close; however, all the problems posed can be dealt with successfully provided appropriate provisions have been made.

Some sub-national groups are, of course, well enough disciplined, sufficiently sophisticated, and have enough financial resources to carry out the operations needed to produce the sort of nuclear device which Carson Mark et al. are considering. And it should be remembered that there are today thousands of people with knowledge of, and experience in, handling nuclear weapons. Some may be recruited to assist in any planned nuclear operations. If no such people can be found who are sympathetic to the aims of the group, there will certainly be some who will co-operate for money.

Very crude nuclear explosives

The nuclear devices considered by Mark et al. are of types similar to those dropped on Nagasaki and Hiroshima. But much cruder designs that will still give a powerful nuclear explosion are possible. These could produce nuclear explosions equivalent to the explosion of between 100 and 1,000 tons of TNT. They might yield several thousand tons, but are unlikely to yield 10,000 tons.

The crudest design could be very easily constructed by a team of technicians (or a competent technician working alone) from, say, a sub-critical mass of plutonium. The plutonium need not be in metal form; plutonium oxide, for example, is more convenient and safer to handle.

The plutonium oxide could be contained in a spherical vessel placed in the centre of a large mass of conventional high explosive, such as TNT. When detonated remotely by an electronic signal the shock wave from the conventional explosive could compress the plutonium enough to produce some nuclear fission.

In a primitive device, no effort would be made to focus the shock wave, and so the high explosive would be simply stacked around the plutonium, probably in the form of a cube. A few detonators would probably be used, arranged to go off simultaneously. The device would easily fit into a medium-sized van.

Even if the explosion from such a crude device was equivalent to the explosion of only a few tens of tons of TNT, it would completely destroy the centre of a relatively large city. The device might, however, explode with a considerably larger explosive power, equivalent to a few hundreds of tons of TNT. Even a thousand tons is not impossible.

For comparison, the largest conventional bomb used in the Second World War used about 10 tons of TNT; it was called the 'earthquake' bomb! An explosion equivalent to that of 100 tons of TNT exploded on the surface would produce a crater about 30 metres across.

In the words of Mason Willrich and Theodore Taylor:

> Under conceivable circumstances, a few people, possibly even one person working alone, who possessed about 10 kilograms of plutonium oxide and a substantial amount of chemical high explosive could, within several weeks, design and build a 'crude fission bomb'. By a 'crude fission bomb' we mean one that would have an excellent chance of exploding with the power of at least 100 tons of chemical high explosive. This could be done using materials and equipment that could be purchased at a hardware store and from commercial suppliers of scientific equipment for student laboratories.
>
> (Willrich and Taylor 1974)

A similar conclusion is drawn by the experts of the Office of Technology Assessment (OTA) of the US Congress. In its publication *Nuclear Proliferation and Safeguards*, the OTA states that:

> A small group of people, none of whom have ever had access to the classified literature, could possibly design and build a crude nuclear explosive device. They would not necessarily require a great deal of technological equipment or have to undertake any experiments. Only modest machine-shop facilities that could be contracted for without arousing suspicion would be required. The financial resources for the acquisition of necessary equipment on open markets need not exceed a fraction of a million dollars. The

group would have to include, at a minimum, a person capable of researching and understanding the literature in several fields and a jack-of-all-trades technician. . . . There is a clear possibility that a clever and competent group could design and construct a device which would produce a significant nuclear yield (i.e. a yield *much* greater than the yield of an equal mass of high explosive).

(*Nuclear Proliferation and Safeguards* 1977)

Nuclear terrorist acts

The fact that a nuclear explosive fabricated by a sub-national group from reactor-grade plutonium will have an unpredictable yield is often used as a main reason why terrorists are unlikely to attempt to acquire nuclear explosives. But this reasoning is incorrect. A sub-national group would normally not need to predict the precise explosive power of any nuclear device it may make. Most likely purposes of the group would be satisfied if the device exploded with a significant nuclear yield.

In this respect, the needs of a sub-national group are quite different from those of the military. The military usually demand to know rather precisely what the yields of their nuclear weapons are likely to be, and would be unwilling to tolerate uncertain yields. Nuclear-weapon designers employed by governments are, therefore, normally required to produce devices which explode with specific yields, predictable to within relatively narrow limits. The weapons must also be very reproducible. The military have very strict requirements for the weapons they are prepared to accept in their arsenals. But a sub-national group would have no such requirements.

Another difference is that the weapons produced for a state's nuclear-weapon programme must satisfy the strictest possible safety conditions. The risk of accidents in which they are subjected to severe mechanical shocks and fires is always there. The weapons must be designed so that if the conventional high explosives are accidentally detonated there is no nuclear fission. A sub-national group, on the other hand, would not have to take into account all conceivable accidents, although it would naturally want to make sure that it could handle its device safely.

Although sub-national groups have not yet used, or credibly threatened to use, nuclear explosives, the very presence of large amounts of plutonium and its frequent transportation may prove to be a temptation that will eventually become irresistible. One or more nuclear explosions set off by terrorists could escalate to a local nuclear war and even to a nuclear world war.

The dangers of nuclear proliferation to sub-national groups are, therefore, similar to those of the spread of nuclear weapons to countries. In practice, they are likely to be significantly greater. If a sub-national group acquired plutonium to make a nuclear explosive, it would be under considerable pressure to construct and detonate the device before the authorities discovered it. Given the extremely sensitive equipment now available to detect nuclear material, the group would have to assume that it would not be long before its nuclear explosive device was discovered.

A primitive nuclear explosive manufactured by a terrorist group, perhaps contained in a vehicle such as a van, could be positioned so that, even if it did not produce any nuclear fission, the explosion of the chemical high explosive would widely disperse the plutonium. Dispersal would be even more widespread if the explosion caused a fire.

The plutonium would be scattered in the form of small particles capable of being inhaled into the lung. Inhaled particles can become embedded in the lung and seriously irradiate surrounding lung tissue. Irradiation by the alpha-particles, given off when plutonium nuclei undergo radioactive decay, can cause lung cancer. Plutonium in particulate form is, therefore, extremely toxic.

Reactor-grade plutonium is actually several times more radioactive than weapons-grade plutonium. This makes it a greater hazard to populations if dispersed. Reactor-grade plutonium is also, of course, far more hazardous than weapons-grade plutonium to people handling it. But, given sensible precautions against achieving criticality accidentally – and thereby producing a very large burst of neutrons – a sub-national group constructing a nuclear explosive from reactor-grade plutonium would not face unmanageable radiological hazards.

Unintentional criticality is the greatest danger facing a sub-national group fabricating a nuclear device from reactor-grade plutonium. But a competent nuclear physicist with the appropriate radiation-monitoring instruments, able to detect neutrons, could make sure that a nuclear explosive device made from reactor-grade plutonium would not explode unintentionally.

The threat of dispersal is perhaps the most likely danger that would follow the illegal acquisition of fissionable material by a sub-national group. The dispersal of some kilograms of the material would make a significant area – of a city, for example – uninhabitable until it had been decontaminated, a process that could take a long time. The very possession by a sub-national group of significant amounts of nuclear material is, therefore, a threat in itself.

A government being blackmailed by a group known to have fissile material would not need to be convinced that the group had the expertise to construct an effective nuclear explosive. The authorities would know that if the device failed to produce a significant nuclear explosion it would almost certainly scatter nuclear material over a large area. And this would be threat enough.

Commenting on this possibility, American ambassador Richard T. Kennedy told a US Congressional hearing that, although the objective of any group or individuals 'who, for political gain, sought to acquire a nuclear weapon' would hopefully be limited to extortion, 'nonetheless the extortion itself is something that cannot be tolerated; it is simply too dangerous a proposition' (*World Commerce in Nuclear Materials* 1987). It is this that makes nuclear threats special. The *mere possession* of fissionable material is likely to be enough to gain the ends of the group that acquires the material.

The nuclear black market

With much fissile material, particularly plutonium, being stored in civilian stockpiles in many countries, and with governments and subnational groups being willing to pay large sums of money for it, the emergence of a black market in nuclear material must be regarded as probable. From time to time, there are stories in the media about the theft of, and attempts to sell, nuclear material. But so far the most reliable of these have involved uranium rather than plutonium. As large amounts of plutonium become available through commercial reprocessing, however, the risk of a plutonium black market obviously grows.

An early example of the illicit acquisition of nuclear material is the smuggling of enriched uranium to Israel between 1962 and 1965. About 100 kilograms of highly enriched uranium disappeared from a factory in Apollo, Pennsylvania, owned by the Nuclear Materials and Equipment Corporation. The factory made fuel elements, containing highly enriched uranium, for nuclear reactors used in American naval warships.

The missing uranium was enough to make about five nuclear weapons. The Central Intelligence Agency (CIA) believe that the uranium went to Israel. At the time, Israel's nuclear reactor at Dimona had not produced enough plutonium to manufacture nuclear weapons.

Evidence collected by researchers for a British television documentary, *The Plutonium Blackmarket*, transmitted by Channel Four on 30 October 1987, suggests that a black market in nuclear material already exists. In the documentary, the former CIA director Admiral Stansfield Turner said: 'I think there has been a black market in fissionable material for nuclear weapons and in the technology. In certain pieces of technology there obviously has been. The Pakistanis have tried to circumvent regulations on export of high-technology materials that are applicable to nuclear weapons and they have been successful in doing that.'

One example of how brazen is the nuclear smuggling to which the Admiral referred has been described by Leonard Spector. In the late 1970s, Albrecht Migule, a West German entrepreneur, 'shipped a nuclear plant to Pakistan in sixty-two truckloads and provided a team of West German engineers to supervise its construction. The facility processes natural uranium into easily gasified uranium hexafluoride so that it can be enriched for possible use in nuclear arms. Thus the plant is a critical building block in Pakistan's nuclear weapons programme' (Spector 1987).

There are many other examples of the smuggling to Pakistan of equipment, special materials, and electronic components from a number of countries, including the Netherlands, Canada and the USA. Other countries, including Israel and, most recently, Iraq, are known to have smuggled items for their nuclear-weapon programmes. All in all, a great deal of nuclear material, equipment, and components for nuclear-weapons programmes have been, and are being, smuggled.

8

CHEMICAL WEAPONS AND WARFARE

Chemical weapons undoubtedly play an important role in international relations. An increasing number of countries are actually or allegedly acquiring these weapons, and allegations of their use continue. But the attitudes of military and political leaders are unclear. Recent events can be interpreted in very different ways.

On the one hand, some military and political leaders are questioning the military effectiveness of chemical weapons. If chemical weapons are no longer perceived to be weapons of mass destruction but, rather, to be of similar status to conventional weapons, they will lose their special deterrent value. The link between chemical and nuclear weapons will be seriously weakened.

This will have serious consequences for countries which believe that their chemical weapons deter the use of nuclear weapons against them. Some Arab countries, for example, have seen their chemical-weapon capability as balancing Israel's nuclear-weapon capability. The perception that chemical weapons do not have a status similar to that of nuclear weapons will have a destabilizing effect in, for example, the Middle East. The conclusion that only nuclear weapons deter nuclear weapons will make some countries determined to acquire nuclear weapons.

The coalition forces during the Gulf War expected the Iraqi forces to use chemical weapons against them, although in the event chemical weapons were not used. But the prospect of a chemical attack did not change the timetable of the coalition's attack. Apparently, troops in modern armies are convinced that protective clothing and gas-masks offer effective protection against chemical weapons.

The military seem to believe that, provided troops are well protected, chemical munitions are, weight for weight, less lethal than modern conventional weapons such as multiple-launch rocket systems firing rockets armed with fragmentation warheads. Moreover, the belief is growing that chemical weapons are relatively ineffective against well-protected populations provided with gas-masks and with access to sealed rooms. But the great lethality of some chemical weapons, such as nerve gases, when used against unprotected populations is not doubted.

Even though there has been a change in perceptions about the utility of chemical weapons, efforts to negotiate a multilateral treaty banning the production, developing and stockpiling of these weapons continue. President Bush has, ever since coming into office, encouraged the negotiation of such a treaty, describing it as an important goal in his foreign policy.

To encourage the negotiation of a multilateral comprehensive ban on chemical weapons, the USA and the USSR negotiated a bilateral agreement, signed by President George Bush and President Mikhail Gorbachev on 1 June 1990, to reduce the huge Soviet and American chemical arsenals. Reductions will, however, be slow and will only take each stockpile down to 5,000 tonnes of chemical-warfare agents – still a considerable arsenal. And it could be the end of the year 2002 before this level is reached. But, under the bilateral agreement, the USA and Russia will cease all production of chemical weapons.

Other countries will, however, continue to produce chemical weapons, and some countries that do not now have chemical weapons plan to acquire them. Before discussing the consequences of these developments it is of interest to consider briefly the history of chemical warfare, to get some idea of the extent of the use of chemical weapons, and the nature of chemical-warfare agents.

Types of chemical weapon

A chemical weapon consists of a chemical agent loaded into a delivery system. The agent is a toxic chemical which attacks the biochemical processes of living organisms. Other weapons, such as incendiary weapons like phosphorus munitions, may release toxic substances but are not regarded as chemical weapons if their main effects do not rely on toxicity.

There are five main categories of chemical-warfare agent: disabling, choking, blister, blood and nerve agents. Chemical-warfare agents may be persistent, staying in the environment for days or even weeks, or non-persistent, which break down quickly.

Toxins, toxic chemicals of biological origin, are classified as both chemical- and biological-warfare agents.

Disabling agents

Disabling, or incapacitating, agents, which include tear gases like CS and CN and arsenicals, are mainly used by police and other forces for riot control. Eye effects and violent vomiting, often induced very rapidly, are the main effect of these compounds.

Chloracetophenone, or CN, is often used in civilian tear-gas weapons. A non-persistent irritant, it is used as an incapacitating agent. Chlorobenzalmalononitrile, or CS, has much stronger effects, causing vomiting, dizziness and breathing difficulties. There is a persistent form of CS which remains active for a few weeks, keeping an area free of people.

Diphenylchloroarsine, or DA, and Adamsite, or DM (10-Chloro-5, 10-dihydrophenarsazine), are arsenicals used in riot control but also early in a chemical-weapon attack. These non-persistent irritants are incapacitating agents, causing violent vomiting almost immediately after exposure. Their military utility is that vomiting prevents exposed troops from putting on gas-masks, making them vulnerable to more lethal chemical agents.

Choking agents

Choking agents attack the respiratory tract, making the membranes swell and the lungs fill with fluid. The victim drowns. Survivors normally suffer chronic breathing problems.

Carbonyl chloride, or phosgene, is a non-persistent, lethal choking agent. It is a colourless gas smelling of new-mown hay. Trichloromethyl chloroformate, or diphosgene, is another non-persistent, lethal choking agent, somewhat more stable than phosgene. The phosgenes have replaced chlorine gas, a chemical-warfare agent used extensively during the First World War. Another important non-persistent, lethal choking agent is chloropicrin (trichloronitromethane).

Blister agents

Blister agents produce large water blisters on exposed skin which heal slowly and may become infected. They may also damage the eyes, blood cells and respiratory tract. Most blister agents have delayed effects which may take up to four hours to emerge.

The most common blister agent is mustard gas, bis(2-chloroethyl) sulphide, also called Yperite. It is a persistent agent, which can be lethal. Mustard gas is an oily liquid, having either a garlic smell or a fishy smell.

Another blister agent is Lewisite, 2-chlorovinyldichloroarsine. A persistent blister agent, which can be lethal, Lewisite has been used in admixture with mustard gas.

Blood agents

Blood agents are absorbed into the body by breathing and kill by entering the bloodstream and, by attacking an enzyme, prevent the synthesis of molecules used by the body as an energy source. Vital organs then cease to function.

Hydrogen cyanide, also called prussic acid, and cyanogen chloride are non-persistent, lethal blood agents. They smell of bitter almonds and kill very quickly – within fifteen minutes or so.

Nerve agents

Nerve gases are in two main groups: the G-agents and the V-agents. G-agents are non-persistent and cause death mainly by inhalation. V-agents, normally liquids, are persistent and can be absorbed through the skin. Nerve agents, which may also enter the body by oral ingestion, are extremely lethal, more potent than any other chemical-warfare agents except toxins.

Nerve gases are typically organophosphorus compounds and are tasteless and colourless. The most lethal ones are: Tabun, GA; Sarin, GB; Soman, GD; and VX. Tabun, Sarin and Soman were discovered by the Germans in the late 1930s and early 1940s. VX was first discovered in Britain.

Tabun is the compound dimethylamido-ethoxy-phosphoryl cyanide; Sarin is isopropoxymethylphosphoryl fluoride; and Soman is pinacoloxymethylphosphoryl fluoride. Soman is much more lethal and rapid in action than Tabun and Sarin. VX is O-ethyl S-(2-(diisopropylamino)-ethyl)methyl-phosphonothioate, and is more persistent and lethal than the G-agents. The lethal dose of the nerve agents for humans is less than 0.01 milligrams per kilogram of body weight.

Soman is semi-persistent and both respiratory and skin-penetrating. Like VX it contaminates the earth and buildings.

Effects of exposure to nerve agents

If you are exposed to any of the nerve gases, it will attack your nervous system. Symptoms develop more slowly when the nerve agents are absorbed through the skin than when inhaled. Soon after a significant exposure, symptoms will occur of increasingly severe damage to the nervous system. These effects occur because nerve gases (like many organophosphorus compounds) inactivate an enzyme in the body called acetylcholinesterase which is essential for the normal functioning of the nervous system.

Nerve impulses are transmitted between nerve fibres and various organs and muscles by the compound acetylcholine. Normally, when acetylcholine has done its job, it is destroyed by acetylcholinesterase, so that the nerve fibres can transmit further impulses. The nerve gas inhibits acetylcholinesterase so that it cannot break down the acetylcholine. The latter accumulates and blocks the nerve function.

The symptoms will include contraction of the pupil of the eye, blurred vision, uncontrollable crying, sweating, nausea, vomiting, urinary incontinence, the accumulation of fluid in the lungs causing severe respiratory distress, loss of bladder and bowel control, and effects on the consciousness ranging from reduced mental capabilities to convulsions, deep coma and, finally, death. Death comes from suffocation, caused by paralysis of the respiratory muscles. A minute drop of a nerve gas, inhaled or absorbed through the skin or eyes, is enough to kill.

Binary chemical weapons

Binaries are an important development in chemical-weapon technology. A binary chemical weapon contains two chemicals. On its own, neither of them is very poisonous. But when they are mixed together they produce a nerve gas.

Isopropanol and methylphosphonyl difluoride, for example, are the two chemical components of an American binary used in 155-millimetre artillery shells. The nerve gas produced is Sarin. The USA has also developed a binary VX spray bomb, called 'Big-eye'.

In a binary weapon, the two chemicals are kept separate until the munition is fired. When it is fired, the chemicals are mixed together, so that when the munition hits its target an aerosol cloud of nerve gas is produced. Before use, one of the chemicals is stored separately. The advantage of binary chemical weapons is that they are easier to store and safer to handle.

Past uses of chemical weapons

Chemical warfare is almost as old as warfare itself. In the fifth century BC, for example, sulphur fumes were used in Greece; and toxic smokes, based on alkaloids and toxins, were described in early Indian and Chinese literature. Arsenic and other poisonous gases were used in the Middle Ages. The Moors allegedly used aconite extracts as poisons on arrowheads against the Spaniards in 1483.

At the end of the fifteenth century, Leonardo da Vinci described the use of toxic smokes, made from a variety of poisons, during sieges and against fortifications. The smoke was typically produced in large fires so that it drifted in a large cloud over the enemy. Toxic smoke warfare was conducted with artillery shells and hand grenades. But chemical warfare as we know it dates from the First World War when, for the first time, the use of chemical weapons had a significant military effect. Poison gases were used to achieve military objectives that could not be attained with other types of weapon.

During the First World War, at least forty-five chemical-warfare agents were used by both sides (the uses of chemical weapons are described in Robinson 1971). A total of about 100 million kilograms of chemicals were used, mainly chlorine, phosgene and mustard gas; they killed a total of about 100,000 people and injured another 1,200,000 or so. About 56,000 of the dead and 420,000 of the wounded were Russian. Serious after-effects, including blindness, tuberculosis, lung cancer, bronchitis and so on, afflicted the survivors, often for the rest of their lives.

Chemical weapons were used by Allied forces against Red forces during the 1919–21 Russian civil war. In the early 1920s, the British Royal Air Force was alleged to have used chemical weapons during peace-keeping operations in the Middle East and in the north-western frontier region of India. And in the mid-1920s the Spanish air force was said to have dropped mustard-gas bombs on Riff rebels in Morocco. Chemical weapons were allegedly used in Manchuria in the early 1930s in battles between Chinese warlords.

Chemical weapons were used by the Italians against the Ethiopians in 1935–6. About 15,000 out of a total of some 50,000 Ethiopian army casualties were caused by chemical weapons (Robinson 1971). Early in the war, Italian aircraft dropped tear-gas grenades on masses of Ethiopian troops. Soon afterwards, mustard-gas bombs were in use. For the rest of the war, mustard gas was normally sprayed from aircraft.

Japan used chemical weapons against Chinese troops and civilians between 1937 and 1945. A wide range of chemical agents were apparently used, including tear gases, phosgene, diphosgene, chloropicrin, hydrogen cyanide, mustard gas and Lewisite. The chemical weapons said to have been used included bombs, artillery shells and toxic candles. The number of Chinese casualties caused by Japanese chemical attacks is not known, but it runs into the thousands. Toxic candles producing clouds of irritant agents were used extensively by the Japanese. In one battle in July 1938, 18,000 toxic candles were lit over a 9-kilometre front to support an infantry attack.

During the Second World War, Hitler's Germany gassed several million Jews and other inmates in at least eight concentration-camps, using mainly carbon monoxide from vehicle exhausts or hydrogen cyanide. The Germans used chemical weapons on one occasion during the Polish campaign. Apparently, mustard-gas bombs were dropped on the suburbs of Warsaw. And there is a report that the Germans used poison gas against Russian troops and civilians in the Crimea.

There were some unintentional releases of chemical agents. During Allied operations at Anzio in early 1943, for example, a German shell hit an Allied dump of chemical weapons and a cloud of chemical-warfare agent drifted towards the German lines.

In the Pacific war, the Japanese used hand grenades containing hydrogen cyanide against American troops on several occasions. But these were small-scale attacks, probably carried out by junior officers and soldiers without permission from the high command.

Apart from the horrific use of gas against defenceless civilian inmates in German concentration-camps, there was little military use of gas in the Second World War. Yet when the war broke out all the belligerents had chemical weapons; by the end of the war the chemical stockpiles were considerably larger than the total amounts of chemical weapons used in the First World War. Moreover, highly lethal nerve agents were available during the Second World War.

Robinson lists a number of allegations of the use of chemical weapons between 1945 and the beginning of the Vietnam War (Robinson 1971). It was alleged that both sides used chemical weapons during the 1945–9 Chinese civil war. In 1947 the French were accused of using gas against Vietnamese rebels, a report denied by France. In 1949, during the Greek civil war, government forces used sulphur dioxide gas, a respiratory irritant, to drive rebels out of caves.

The Americans were accused of using chemical weapons on several occasions during the 1951–2 Korean War. Cuban government troops were alleged to have used mustard-type chemical agents against guerrilla forces in 1957. French forces were alleged to have used poison gas against Algerian rebels in 1957. French and Spanish forces were accused by the Moroccan Saharan rebels of making a chemical attack on Rio de Oro in 1958. Also in 1958, the Chinese government accused the Chinese Nationalist forces on Quemoy of bombarding troops of the Chinese People's Army on the mainland with artillery shells containing chemical weapons.

Apart from the incident in Greece in 1949, none of the allegations of the use of chemical weapons between 1945 and 1963 has been credibly substantiated. The allegations that chemical weapons were used between 1963 and 1967 by Egyptian forces during their intervention in the civil war in the Yemen are, however, widely believed. Mustard gas and phosgene were reportedly used. According to SIPRI, casualties caused by a half of the alleged incidents 'amounted to at least 1,400 dead and about 900 severely gassed'.

In 1965 the Kurdish Democratic Party claimed that the Iraqi army used an unidentified gas against Kurdish forces – the first allegation, denied by the Iraqi government, of Iraqi use of chemical weapons against the Kurds. The reported purchase of gas-masks by the Iraqi government added credibility to the Kurdish allegations.

Portuguese troops were accused of using gas against rebels in Guinea-Bissau in 1968. And Israeli forces were accused of using poison gas against Palestinian guerrillas in the Jordan valley in 1969.

A more modern form of chemical warfare is the military use of plant-killing agents (herbicides) to clear wooded areas by defoliation and to destroy food crops. Herbicides have, of course, civilian uses, particularly in agriculture and forestry. But the substances were developed from chemical-warfare research during the Second World War.

The first military use of modern anti-plant chemicals was probably their use by British forces against nationalist guerrillas in Malaya in the 1950s. The Portuguese were also accused of using anti-crop chemicals in Angola in 1970 against insurgents' food crops.

But these uses were extremely modest compared with the extensive and systematic use of anti-plant agents by the American military in Vietnam between 1961 and 1975 during what has become known as the Second Indo-China War. The massive herbicidal programme carried out by the USA over a period of more than a decade has been described by Westing (Westing 1976).

The USA sprayed a volume of more than 18 million gallons, containing almost 55 million kilograms of active herbicides, mainly on the forests of South Vietnam but also on its crops. About half a million gallons of herbicides were sprayed on Laos. Three main anti-plant agents were used, code-named Orange, White and Blue. Agent Blue killed by desiccation – by preventing a plant from retaining its moisture. Agents Orange and White killed by interfering with the normal metabolism of the sprayed plants by mimicking plant hormones. About 95 per cent of the volume of the agents was sprayed from C–130 transport aircraft flying not far above tree-top level. Most of the rest was sprayed from helicopters.

Westing estimates that anti-plant warfare in Vietnam virtually obliterated more than 50,000 hectares of South Vietnamese inland forests. In addition, about 1.3 million hectares of upland forests (12 per cent of South Vietnam's total forest) were partially destroyed, experiencing up to 50 per cent tree mortality.

Coastal mangroves, a major source of small timbers, charcoal, fish and other products, were also attacked with anti-plant agents. About 124,000 hectares, or 41 per cent, of South Vietnam's mangrove habitat were utterly destroyed, leaving this huge area essentially lifeless.

An inadvertent consequence of this form of chemical warfare was the dissemination across South Vietnam of dioxin, an impurity of

Agent Orange, the most widely and heavily used of the three herbicides. According to Westing, a total of about 170 kilograms of dioxin was scattered over about 1 million hectares. About half of this dioxin decomposed within a few days, but the other half became incorporated into the environment, decomposing with a half-life of about 3.5 years. Because dioxin is very toxic, having carcinogenic and genetic effects on humans, there may well be long-term health effects on the indigenous population of Vietnam and on American troops involved in spraying Agent Orange.

During the second half of the 1970s there were allegations that Laotian and Vietnamese forces used mustard gas, irritants and nerve gases in aircraft attacks on rebels in Laos between 1974 and 1981. It was also alleged that mycotoxins were used in these attacks – the first time that these substances were mentioned as chemical-warfare agents. The American government also accused the Soviet forces of using mycotoxins, and nerve gas and irritants, against mujahedin forces in Afghanistan between 1979 and 1981. During the same period, Vietnamese forces were alleged to have used mycotoxins, together with nerve gas, irritants and cyanide, in Kampuchea.

The American allegation that the Soviet Union and its allies were using toxin weapons in South-East Asia and Afghanistan was serious because, if true, it would be a violation of the Biological Weapon Convention. The USA alleged that a new type of chemical toxin weapon had been developed based on mycotoxins, which are poisons produced naturally by fungi. These toxins, which are chemicals produced biologically, are said to be the agents in the 'yellow rain' reported by refugees from Laos and Kampuchea. Mycotoxins are also said to have been found on Soviet gas-masks captured in Afghanistan.

In a typical attack described, for example, by Hmong people who had lived in the Laotian Highlands, an attacking aircraft would release a cloud, often yellow in colour, that would descend on a village. Those exposed to yellow rain were said to experience, very soon after exposure, a range of symptoms, including violent itching, vomiting, dizziness and distorted vision. It was claimed that some casualties died within an hour, from shock and massive bleeding from the stomach. These symptoms are typical of those produced by some fungus poisons.

The American allegations have, however, not generally been supported by scientific evidence. An analysis, by Australian and British scientists, for example, of samples of leaves and pebbles said to be contaminated with yellow rain and collected from refugees who had fled to Thailand concluded that the samples consisted of yellow pollen grains from local rainforests. A United Nations expert group has also studied the evidence and concluded: 'While the group could not state that these allegations had been proven, nevertheless it could not disregard the circumstantial evidence suggestive of the possible use of some sort of toxic chemical substance in some instances.'

An alternative explanation, supported by academic studies, is that 'yellow rain' is not a product of mycotoxin warfare but arises from mass-defecation flights by wild honey-bees (Lundin *et al.* 1988). Fungus spores may land on the pollen-filled faeces dropped by the bees in flight and produce natural mycotoxins. Although most experts support the view that the mycotoxins were produced naturally, the controversy has not been satisfactorily resolved.

During the 1980s, Ethiopian forces were alleged to have used chemical weapons against Eritrean secessionists and against Somali forces; Indonesian forces allegedly used chemical weapons in East Timor; Soviet-made nerve-gas weapons were reportedly used in the Angolan war against UNITA rebels; Libyan forces were accused of using poison gas in northern Chad; and, in April 1989, Soviet police used a riot-control agent – chloracetophenone (CN) – against demonstrators in Georgia, causing some deaths and injuries. But the most serious chemical-weapon attacks occurred during the Iran–Iraq War between 1983 and 1988.

Iraq used chemical weapons on frequent occasions against Iranian military forces during the war. This use was established beyond all reasonable doubt by international scientific missions sent to the war zones by the United Nations. The evidence shows that Iraq used mustard gas and nerve gas against Iranian troops on several occasions (Lundin 1989). There is evidence that Iran used mustard gas, but not nerve gas, against Iraqi forces. Iran, however, has strenuously denied the use of chemical weapons. The number of victims of chemical warfare in the Iran–Iraq War is not known, but some estimates imply that the number of casualties is in the tens of thousands, possibly many tens of thousands.

Iraq also used chemical weapons against its Kurdish civilians, most notably at Halabja in March 1988. About 5,000 Kurds died and 7,000 were injured at Halabja (Lundin 1989).

In summary, allegations of the use of chemical weapons abound. In a large fraction of the 200 or so conflicts since the Second World War, one side or the other has accused its enemy of making chemical attacks on it. But the evidence for the bulk of these allegations is flimsy indeed.

Chemical weapons were certainly used in the First World War, and by Britain and the White Army in Russia during the Russian civil war. Between the world wars, they were used by the Italians in the Ethiopia war and by Japan against China. They were probably used by the British against Afghans in 1919. During the Second World War, gas was used to exterminate millions of Jews in German concentration-camps.

Since 1945 the Americans conducted extensive anti-plant warfare in South Vietnam and Laos, and Iraq used chemical weapons against Iranian forces and its own Kurdish citizens. And there are strong reasons to believe that Egypt used chemical weapons in the Yemen. Apart from these uses, other allegations must be treated with great caution.

9

THE SPREAD OF CHEMICAL WEAPONS

Only three countries are definitely known to have chemical weapons: the USA, Russia and Iraq. Most experts believe that France has them, although official statements are ambiguous. And according to official American statements, based on intelligence assessments, between twenty and thirty Third World countries have chemical weapons or the capability to produce them if they took the political decision to do so. Iran, Libya and Syria have been named in these statements as having chemical weapons, but the other countries in the list have not been named.

The American chemical arsenal

The USA has not officially announced the size of its chemical arsenal, but the best estimates put it at about 35,000 tons of agents. Stocks are held at eight locations in the USA and on Johnston Atoll in the Pacific.

Until the end of 1990, the USA had deployed chemical weapons in its munitions depot at Clausen in the western part of Germany. This stockpile, which was returned to the USA, consisted of 400 tonnes of nerve agents in about 120,000 artillery shells. The shells, for 155-millimetre and 203-millimetre (8-inch) howitzers, weighed about 7,000 tonnes. It was said that these artillery shells represented about 1 per cent of the total American supply of chemical weapons (Lundin and Stock 1991).

Until its 1990 bilateral agreement with the USSR, the USA planned to deploy about 9,000 tonnes of binary agents in 'Big-eye' aircraft bombs and artillery shells. In January 1988, President Reagan gave approval for the production of Big-eye bombs and in fiscal year 1988 Congress funded the production of both binary bombs and artillery shells. These programmes have been cancelled now that the bilateral agreement prohibits the production of chemical weapons. But the Pentagon seems to be continuing with the development of binary chemical warheads for strategic cruise missiles and for the multiple-launch rockets system (MLRS).

In addition, the Pentagon hopes to develop two new types of chemical-warfare agent. One is an agent that penetrates gas-masks and protective clothing to make such protection ineffective. The other is a non-lethal agent that incapacitates very rapidly – a sort of 'knock-out gas'.

The agents in today's American chemical-warfare arsenal include: Sarin nerve gas; binary Sarin nerve gas; VX nerve gas; and mustard gas. In addition, chemical weapons designed for close combat include the agents CN and CS (Lundin and Stock 1991).

Sarin is contained in 105-millimetre, 155-millimetre and 8-inch (203-millimetre) artillery shells. Binary Sarin is contained in artillery shells. Mustard gas is contained in 4.2-inch mortars. Aircraft bombs contain Sarin. Aircraft sprays contain Sarin and VX. The arsenal also includes land mines containing VX and hand grenades containing CS and CN.

The bulk, some 94 per cent, of the American chemical arsenal is kept in the USA, in eight army sites (Aberdeen, Maryland; Anniston, Alabama; Lexington-Blue Grass, Kentucky; Newport, Indiana; Pine Bluff, Arkansas; Pueblo, Colorado; Tooele, Utah; and Umatilla, Oregon). The remainder is at Johnston Atoll.

When Congress authorized the development of binary chemical weapons, in November 1985, it required the Pentagon to destroy existing American chemical stockpiles. In addition, the 1990 American–Soviet bilateral agreement requires each side to begin destruction of declared chemical stockpiles by the end of 1992; to destroy at least 50 per cent of them by the end of 1999; and to reduce them to 5,000 tonnes of chemical-warfare agents by 2002.

To carry out this destruction programme, called the US Chemical Weapons Demilitarization Program, the USA is to build a destruction facility, using a high-temperature incinerator, near each of the eight stockpile sites in the USA and near the one at Johnston Atoll. This construction programme began on Johnston Atoll in 1988 and at Tooele in October 1989; it should be completed by mid-1994. Actual disposal operations of chemical weapons began in 1990 and are scheduled to be completed by the end of 1998.

The destruction of large stockpiles of chemical weapons is today a difficult and politically sensitive task because of the potential environmental impact. The problem is particularly difficult because, apart from binary weapons, no thought was given to destruction when the weapons were designed. The transport of chemical weapons, particularly aged ones, is also a major problem, with considerable environmental ramifications.

When environmental issues raised little public interest, chemical weapons were simply dumped at sea. For example, some 35,000 tonnes of old chemical munitions from the First World War were dumped in the North Sea, off Zeebrugge, Belgium, and as much as 150,000 tonnes of chemical munitions were dumped in the Skagerrak off the west coast of Sweden after the Second World War. Many other examples of sea-dumping could be given. This method of disposal, however convenient for the authorities, is simply no longer publicly acceptable.

Today, it is most desirable to destroy chemical stocks at the places where they are stored. The Americans currently destroy chemical weapons by incinerating the chemical agent and decontaminating the munition. The Russians prefer a thermochemical neutralization process.

The ex-Soviet chemical arsenal

Until 1987, the USSR denied that it had any chemical weapons. President Gorbachev then said that the USSR had stopped making chemical weapons and that a destruction plant was being built in the Soviet Union. In January 1989, the then Soviet Foreign Minister, Eduard Shevardnadze, confirmed that the USSR was not producing chemical weapons, and stated that it had none outside its territory, and had never transferred them to any other country.

Later in 1989, under Gorbachev's *glasnost* policy, the Soviet Foreign Minister announced that the net weight of the chemical-warfare agents in the Soviet stockpile did not exceed 50,000 tonnes. In 1990 the Soviet Union officially announced that its 'stockpiles of toxic substances exceeds US stockpiles by 10,000 tonnes' and that this excess was accumulated before 1945.

The official American and British estimates of the size of the Soviet chemical arsenal were much higher than the Soviets have admitted, suggesting that the Soviets had at least 300,000 tons of chemical-warfare agents. Also, the British government maintained in 1989 that the USSR had not stopped producing and testing chemical weapons.

The difference in these figures may arise from the definition of chemical weapons. The 300,000 tonnes estimate may include 'weapons that have already been manufactured, and munitions and materials assembled for making weapons'. If this is so – and there is some evidence from British intelligence sources that it is – both the Soviet figure of 50,000 tonnes, which applied only to the weight of chemical-warfare agents in the arsenal, and the British and American estimates of 300,000 tonnes, which then includes the weights of agents and munitions, may be right. Be this as it may, in late 1989 the Central

Intelligence Agency reduced its estimate of the size of the Soviet chemical stockpile from 300,000 to 75,000 tonnes (Lundin 1990).

Another example of *glasnost* was the invitation to governmental disarmament experts, of countries participating in the Conference on Disarmament in Geneva, and journalists to visit the chemical-weapon testing-ground at Shikhany and the chemical-weapon destruction facility being built at Chapayevsk in Kazakhstan. The visit took place in October 1987.

The Soviet chemical weapons displayed at Shikhany were: Sarin nerve agent contained in 122-millimetre, 130-millimetre and 152-millimetre artillery shells; VX nerve agent contained in 130-millimetre and 152-millimetre artillery shells; Thickened Lewisite contained in 122-millimetre artillery shells; Sarin nerve agent contained in 122-millimetre, 140-millimetre and 240-millimetre artillery rockets; VX nerve agent in 122-millimetre artillery rockets; Mustard and Lewisite mixture in 100-kilogram aircraft bombs; Sarin nerve agent in 100-kilogram and 250-kilogram aircraft bombs; VX in 540-millimetre tactical missile warheads; Thickened VX in 884-millimetre tactical missile warheads; Thickened Soman in 250-kilogram spray tanks; Mustard and Lewisite mixture in 250-kilogram and 1,500-kilogram spray tanks; and CS in hand grenades. The weight of the munitions varied from 0.25-kilogram hand grenades to 963-kilogram spray tanks, and the agent-fill varied in weight from 0.17 kilograms in each hand grenade to 630-kilograms in each of the largest spray tanks.

The Soviets claimed that the munitions displayed included all the types in the existing chemical arsenal. The 1985 US Defense Intelligence Agency Report claimed that, in addition to these types, the Soviet chemical arsenal contained warheads for cruise missiles, warheads for long- and medium-range ballistic missiles, land mines and mortar rounds. The Report also claimed that, in addition to the agents displayed at Shikhany, the Soviet arsenal included phosgene, hydrogen cyanide, tabun nerve agent, and psychochemical agents.

During the Shikhany visit the Soviets demonstrated a mobile unit for the destruction of chemical weapons. But it was only suitable for small-scale destruction. Because of public concern about environmental effects, the larger (although still relatively small, being able to destroy up to 500 tonnes a year) facility at Chapayevsk has not been put into use. The Russians may build a small number of automated destruction facilities in sparsely populated areas, but a final decision about a chemical-weapon destruction programme has yet to be taken.

The French chemical arsenal

On 29 September 1988, President Mitterrand told the United Nations General Assembly that France 'has no chemical weapons'. But most experts believe that, in fact, France has a chemical arsenal containing a few hundred tonnes of chemical-warfare agents. It is also believed that France has developed binary weapons but has not yet decided to deploy them.

That France has chemical weapons is likely given France's intention, also expressed by President Mitterrand, to deploy any types of weapon held by other powers, including chemical weapons. An explanation of the controversy about France's chemical capability 'might be that France had not weaponized its bulk stockpiles of chemical warfare agents, that is, had not filled munitions with them' (Lundin 1989). President Mitterrand's denial may, in other words, be a matter of definition.

The proliferation of chemical weapons

There is considerable concern about the rate at which other countries may be acquiring chemical weapons. We do not know for sure which countries have chemical weapons. The uncertainty arises because any country with a significant agro-chemical or pharmaceutical industry could produce chemical weapons if it chose to do so. This means, of course, that virtually all industrialized countries and many Third World countries have the expertise and industrial capacity to produce chemical-warfare agents.

Nerve agents, for example, are organophosphorus compounds, similar to pesticides. A producer of pesticides could rather easily also produce nerve agents. And, of course, a country intent on setting up a plant to produce chemical-warfare agents clandestinely could disguise it as a pesticide plant.

The production of mustard gas is particularly easy to disguise. The main chemicals in its production are thiodiglycol and hydrogen chloride. Thiodiglycol is extensively used in the pharmaceutical industry and is relatively easy to acquire; hydrogen chloride is a very common chemical compound, the production of which is impossible to control. If a country was unable to obtain thiodiglycol in sufficient quantities, it could make it itself from chloroethanol, a commonly used chemical in the pharmaceutical and agro-chemical industries.

The technology of most chemical munitions is relatively well known and should give little trouble to countries able to produce chemical-warfare agents. Chemical munitions include grenades, artillery and mortar shells, land mines, multiple-launch rocket systems, aircraft bombs, warheads for missiles of all ranges, bomblets and cluster weapons. The munition converts the payload of chemical-warfare agent it carries into a cloud of particles or vapour or an aerosol of droplets. In an artillery shell, for example, a cylinder of high explosive, with an appropriate fuse and detonator, is aligned along the axis of the shell which is then filled with the agent. When the explosive goes off the agent is dispersed – a relatively simple process.

Recent statements, particularly by President George Bush, imply that the major powers are anxious to prevent the further proliferation of chemical weapons. But the actions of these powers are sometimes not consistent with this policy.

For example, there was very little international criticism of Iraq for using chemical weapons against Iranian forces during the Iran-Iraq war. This fact, and the undoubted military advantage gained by Iraq over Iran by the use of chemical weapons, was, of course, noted by all countries and may well have persuaded some of them to acquire a chemical-weapon capability.

The lack of criticism is all the more serious because the use of chemical weapons by Iraq is without doubt a blatant violation of international law. Iraq is a party to the 1925 Geneva Protocol prohibiting the use and asphyxiating, poisonous or other gases and of bacteriological methods of warfare. Actually, all nations are, according to most international lawyers, bound by the Protocol because a ban on the first use of chemical weapons has become a well-established customary international law, binding both on parties and non-parties.

An important characteristic of chemical weapons is that small nations can produce them relatively easily and cheaply in amounts which may, in the region, be strategically significant. This is why chemical weapons are seen by many as potential weapons of mass destruction for smaller countries – 'poor countries' atom bombs'. This adds to the current concern about the danger that such weapons may proliferate. It should, however, be emphasized that after the Gulf War the military utility of chemical weapons is being questioned. This may reduce the enthusiasm for, and therefore the spread of, these weapons.

Iraq

Before their August 1990 invasion of Kuwait, the Iraqis were producing mustard gas and nerve agents. The main production site was at Samarra and was called the Muthanna State Establishment or the State Enterprise for Pesticide Production (Sigmund and Sigmund, October 1991). It was heavily damaged by bombing during the Gulf War. A team of experts from the United Nations Special Commission visited the site after the war and found it to be 170 square kilometres in area;

the major facilities occupied some 25 square kilometres. The team found mustard gas and Sarin (GB) and GF nerve agents, and evidence of the presence of impure Tabun (GA), used in the Iran–Iraq War. It appears that the site had been used for the production of two herbicides, and that research had been performed on Soman (GD) and VX nerve gases but that these agents had not been produced on a large scale. The facility could produce 2.5 tons of Sarin and 5 tons of mustard gas a day. The total Iraqi chemical-weapon stockpile is estimated to have been about 2,000 tonnes of agent, including some 400 tons of mustard gas and 150 tons of nerve agents, mostly Sarin but also some GF and Tabun, and large amounts of tear gas, mostly CS.

The Iraqis were able to deliver chemical weapons by artillery shells and aircraft bombs. They also apparently had chemical land mines and, according to a statement made to the United Nations after the war about their remaining chemical weapons, they had some warheads containing chemical weapons for their Scud ground-to-ground missiles.

Other countries

There are reasons to suspect that Middle East countries, other than Iraq, possessing chemical weapons include Egypt, Iran, Israel, Libya and Syria. Israel's Science Minister, Yuval Neeman, said in June 1990, when commenting on Iraqi threats to attack Israel with chemical weapons, that Israel had the chemical-weapons capability to respond to the Iraqi threats. It would be extremely surprising if it hadn't. According to a CIA assessment the Israeli production of mustard and nerve gases began in the 1970s.

Iraq accused Iran of using chemical weapons several times against Iraqi forces during the Iran-Iraq War. If true, these allegations mean, of course, that Iran possesses chemical weapons. Iran itself has made contradictory statements about a chemical-weapon capability, implying on several occasions that it has a chemical-weapon production capability. Iran has certainly tried to purchase chemicals, like thiodiglycol, that could be used to produce chemical-warfare agents.

American officials frequently stated during the late 1980s that Libya has constructed a chemical-weapons plant at Rabta. Libya responded that the plant, built with assistance from Austrian, Italian, Japanese, Thai and West German companies, was for the production of agro-chemicals. The USA threatened to bomb the plant, which was reported to have burned down in 1989.

It was later claimed that the fire was faked to distract attention from the construction of another chemical-weapon plant at the Sebha Oasis. It is of interest to note that, while the USA was strongly criticizing

Libya for making, or preparing to make, chemical weapons, it was ignoring Iraq's growing chemical-weapon capability.

Little is known about Syria's chemical-weapon capability. The Syrian chemical-weapon plant is said to be located in a remote desert site north of Damascus. Initially, Syria reportedly imported chemical weapons from the USSR. The Soviets were also accused of assisting Syria in developing chemical weapons but denied having done so.

But Syria is now apparently producing indigenously chemical agents, including lethal nerve gases, and the warheads to deliver them, including warheads that can be fitted to Scud-B and SS-21 surface-to-surface missiles. Syria would, of course, also have the option of using aircraft to deliver bombs filled with chemical-warfare agents.

Egypt is thought to be the first country in the Middle East to have chemical weapons. As we have seen, Egyptian forces probably used chemical weapons during their intervention in the Yemeni civil war. And it is reported that Israeli troops captured Egyptian stocks of nerve gas in the Sinai in the 1967 Six-Day War.

The Egyptians may have acquired British chemical weapons left behind when British forces departed from Egypt in 1952. German rocket scientists were employed in the 1970s by President Nasser's administration to build missiles for Egypt. According to some reports, warheads filled with chemical-warfare agents were fabricated for these missiles. Allegations were made in 1989 that Egypt was building a chemical-weapon production plant – reports denied by President Mubarak.

African countries suspected of possessing chemical weapons include Angola, Ethiopia, Somalia, South Africa and Sudan. Angolan forces allegedly acquired various types of chemical weapon from the Soviet Union. Somalia and Sudan are said to have acquired chemical weapons from Libya.

Asian countries said to possess chemical weapons include Afghanistan, Burma, India, North Korea, Pakistan, the Philippines, Taiwan, Thailand and Vietnam. Latin American countries suspected of possessing chemical weapons include Argentina, Chile, Cuba and El Salvador.

A number of these countries have made official declarations of non-possession of chemical weapons: Afghanistan, Argentina, Burma, Egypt, Ethiopia, India, Pakistan, South Africa and Vietnam. But ambiguities about definitions make these declarations difficult to evaluate. For example, sometimes a country will say it opposes the possession of chemical weapons but does not say whether or not it possesses them. Or a country may say that it does not have chemical weapons but does not say whether it is deploying chemical weapons of an ally.

Chemical terrorism

'Terrorists' access to chemical and biological weapons is a growing threat to the international community. There are no insurmountable technical obstacles that would prevent terrorist groups from using chemical weapons.' This grim warning was given by George Shultz, the US Secretary of State, on 7 January, 1989 in his speech to the International Chemical Disarmament Conference in Paris.

Up to then, the authorities had been extremely reluctant even to talk about terrorists' access to weapons of mass destruction – nuclear, chemical or biological. Shultz decided to break the taboo because the CIA believed that Libya was producing chemical weapons and feared that it would give them to terrorist groups like the IRA or an anti-Arafat Palestinian splinter group. Presumably, these CIA fears still apply.

If terrorists manufacture weapons of mass destruction in the near future, they are likely to opt for chemical rather than biological or nuclear weapons. Chemical terrorism is of considerable current concern because it is relatively easy to find out, from the open literature, how to make chemical-warfare agents, including nerve gas, get the chemicals required to do so, and then prepare the agent.

Tabun

Of all the chemical-warfare agents, the most attractive for terrorists are likely to be the nerve gases because of their high lethality. Of the nerve gases, Tabun is the easiest to make and is, therefore, the most likely candidate for chemical terrorism. Tabun is prepared in two stages. First, dimethylamido-phosphoryl dichloride is prepared from dimethylamine and phosphoryl chloride. In the second stage, Tabun is prepared from dimethylamidophosphoryl dichloride and sodium cyanide in the presence of ethyl alcohol. Details of the method of preparation are openly available.

It is not difficult to buy on the open market moderate quantities of the chemicals used in the preparation (which include dimethylamine, sodium cyanide and phosphoryl chloride) even though relatively large quantities of phosphoryl chloride are needed. It takes ten times as much phosphoryl chloride to produce a given amount of Tabun.

If terrorists were nervous about buying the precursor chemicals, they could make them. They could make dimethylamine, for example, by simply mixing methanol and ammonia. These chemicals are easier to get hold of than dimethylamine, and their purchase would give rise to less suspicion.

Anyone that can handle chemicals reasonably competently can make

Tabun. You would not need very special chemical apparatus to do so, although the preparation should take place, with stringent precautions, in a fume-cupboard. In the first stage, for example, the solution is boiled for some hours in an atmosphere of carbon dioxide. Some distillation has to be done *in vacuo*. And, of course, the final compound must soon be transferred to a sealed container! But these are not difficult problems for a competent chemist.

A reasonably sophisticated terrorist group would have little difficulty in having enough Tabun made to kill a large number of people. If the group did not have chemists among its members, it could find qualified sympathizers or hire them.

A terrorist group would, in fact, need only a small volume of a nerve gas. A fraction of a litre of nerve agent would, therefore, give a terrorist group an enormous killing power.

Currently, it would be virtually impossible to prevent terrorists getting hold of the chemicals needed to produce such quantities of nerve gas. Anyone can buy enough of the chemicals, with no questions asked.

Dispersal

Having made the nerve gas, a terrorist group would need to disperse it. Again, the technology for dispersal is not difficult. Terrorists could, for example, make or acquire a device to produce an aerosol so that the nerve gas could be released as a cloud of droplets. The device could be placed so that the aerosol cloud passes into, say, a city's underground-train tunnel system. If the aerosol was set off during the rush hour, which could be done by a timer or by a remote-control device, a very large number of people would probably be killed. Alternatively, if the nerve gas were injected into the air-conditioning or ventilation system of a large building it would probably kill a large fraction of the people in the building.

10

BIOLOGICAL WARFARE

Most people think of biological and chemical warfare as similar types of warfare. They are usually thought of as more revolting and unacceptable than any other form of warfare, except perhaps nuclear war. Biological warfare is generally considered to be more odious than chemical warfare.

As we have seen, allegations of the use of chemical weapons in modern times abound but the evidence for the vast majority of them is slim indeed. In fact, there have been very few *militarily significant* uses of chemical warfare. And this applies even more to modern biological weapons. Although there have been many allegations of their use, not one has been convincingly proved. The strongest evidence by far relates to some use of biological weapons by the Japanese in the early 1940s during their war against China.

But we must conclude that so far there has been no *militarily significant* use of modern biological weapons in armed conflict. This must not be taken to mean that biological weapons are of no importance. On the contrary. The potential use of modern biological weapons as effective weapons of mass destruction gives them considerable significance in international affairs, a significance that may well be enhanced by developments in genetic engineering.

Past uses of biological weapons

Activities that can be considered to be forms of biological warfare have, however, a long history. These mainly involve the use of pathogens for sabotage. Perhaps the oldest form of biological warfare was the contamination of wells and reservoirs of drinking water with human and animal corpses. People often had no other choice but to drink the water and many became diseased, particularly if the corpses in the well were infected.

Robinson mentions examples of this tactic from early Persian, Greek and Roman literature and down to 'innumerable European wars, the

American Civil War, the South African Boer Wars' (Robinson 1971). Infected corpses were also catapulted into cities under siege. In the fourteenth century, for example, plague was introduced in this way into cities under siege. According to Robinson, this technique was used until 1710 when the Russians besieged Swedish troops during the battle of Reval and caused a plague epidemic by throwing bodies infected with plague over the city walls.

In 1763 the British spread smallpox during wars against the native Indians of North America, using contaminated blankets./The British got a taste of their own medicine when the Americans used smallpox against them during the Revolutionary War.

A modern example of such use of biological agents occurred in Brazil where landowners were brought to trial for deliberately spreading smallpox and other diseases among Indian tribes in the Mato Grosso between 1957 and 1963. The landowners wanted the Indians removed from rubber-producing areas.

Unlike chemical weapons, biological weapons were not used in battle during the First World War. There is some suggestion that the Germans attempted to infect horses with glanders and cattle with anthrax. The evidence for the former is somewhat stronger than that for the latter, but is not convincing.

It is widely believed that biological weapons were used by the Japanese army during the Second World War: as sabotage weapons against the Soviet Union and Mongolia during 1939–40; in air attacks against Chinese cities between 1940 and 1944; and against Chinese troops in 1942 (Robinson 1971). There are reports of plague bacilli being dropped by Japanese aircraft in raids on several Chinese cities. In some cases, the Japanese were reported to have spread plague bacteria by human fleas (*Pulex irritans*). In 1949 a Soviet military court at Khaborovsk tried twelve Japanese soldiers, including the commander of the Kwantung army, for using biological weapons against Chinese troops and civilians and for using prisoners of war as subjects in biological-warfare experiments.

The Japanese undoubtedly had a large research and development programme in biological warfare, run by a unit of the Kwantung army called Department 731. Directed by General Shiro Ishii, mainly from a base at Pingfan, South Manchuria, it employed over 3,000 scientists, technicians and military personnel. Several thousand others worked in eighteen outstations scattered throughout Japanese-controlled territory.

Japanese scientists investigated several diseases as potential biological-warfare agents, including anthrax, brucellosis, glanders, tuberculosis and typhoid. During their research they deliberately infected thousands of prisoners of war, mainly Chinese and Soviet, a large fraction of whom died in agony. The Japanese biological-warfare research programme was justified by allegations that Soviet spies had used bacteria, particularly anthrax, in sabotage missions into Kwantung province in 1935.

A Japanese intelligence report alleges that between 1937 and 1939, during the Japan-China conflict, the Chinese sabotaged water supplies and food supplies on a number of occasions by contaminating them with anthrax and cholera.

Between 1951 and 1953, during the Korean War, the Chinese, Soviet and North Korean communist authorities kept up a continuous stream of accusations that the American military was using biological weapons against targets in North Korea and China, accusations strongly denied by the American government. The human diseases alleged to have been used were anthrax, cholera, encephalitis, meningitis and plague. In addition, American forces were alleged to have spread animal and plant diseases. Diseases were said to have been spread by insects, ticks and small rodents, usually dropped by aircraft.

Boserup et al. analysed in detail the reports of American use in biological agents during the Korean War to illustrate the extremely difficult problem of verifying allegations of use (Boserup et al. 1971). They point out that 'whether the allegations are true or false, they caused the United States a loss of international good-will, even though US requests for impartial investigation were rejected'.

The story is important because it demonstrated the power of allegations of the use of biological weapons to stimulate public opinion. To obtain the propaganda value of such allegations is an obvious motive for making them. This may well explain some of the allegations made since the Korean War. Surprisingly, though, there were no significant allegations of the use of biological weapons by either side during the 1961–75 Vietnam War.

A typical example of a probably propagandistic allegation is the accusation made by the Cuban government that America's Central Intelligence Agency used biological agents in Cuba to spread haemorrhagic dengue and haemorrhagic conjunctivitis in humans and to cause sugar-cane rust, blue mould of tobacco, and African swine fever. The accusations were strenuously denied by the American government. Another example is the accusation in 1970 by the South Korean government that North Korea had caused the epidemic of cholera that struck south-western Korea in 1969.

Biological-warfare agents

Biological-warfare agents are disease-carrying substances and organisms. Possible agents include: bacteria, like plague; viruses, such as yellow fever; rickettsiae (bacteria-like bodies found in the tissues of lice, ticks, mites and fleas which cause disease, like typhus, when transmitted to humans); and fungi, like coccidioidomycosis. Lethal agents considered suitable for biological warfare include: plague; typhus; smallpox; Rocky Mountain spotted fever; cholera; glanders; Eastern encephalitis; Japanese encephalitis; St Louis encephalitis; Russian spring–summer encephalitis; Argentinian haemorrhagic fever; Bolivian haemorrhagic fever; Crimean–Congo haemorrhagic fever; Korean haemorrhagic fever; Marburg disease; Ebola haemorrhagic fever; yellow fever; anthrax; melioidosis; and tularemia (rabbit fever). Incapacitating biological-warfare agents include: Chikungunya fever; Venezuelan equine encephalomyelitis; brucellosis; Western encephalitis; dengue haemorrhagic fever; Lassa fever; lymphocytic choriomeningitis; hepatitis; Rift Valley fever; and Q fever.

The American biological-weapon stockpile which was destroyed, in 1971 and 1972, under the Biological Weapon Convention included at the time of destruction: lethal agents causing anthrax and tularemia; incapacitating agents causing Q fever and Venezuelan equine encephalomyelitis; and anti-plant agents causing rice blast and black stem rust of wheat. In addition, the stockpile earlier contained a lethal agent causing yellow fever and an incapacitating agent causing brucellosis.

Anthrax is the favourite lethal biological-warfare agent. It is relatively very easy to culture in large quantities, easy to disseminate, and, most important, a very hardy pathogen. It can infect both humans and animals, including cows, sheep, horses and pigs.

Anthrax is particularly suitable for dissemination by aerosol because it forms spores which have a protective coating that protects the active material. Not only does this make anthrax bacteria able to survive the rigours of aerosolization, but it also gives them a long lifetime after dissemination. Anthrax spores live for days even in direct sunlight; in soils they can survive for decades. The British tested an anthrax biological weapon on the deserted Gruinard Island in 1942. It was forty years before the island was safe to visit.

Anthrax kills almost all untreated patients. Robinson *et al.* describe the progress of the disease: 'After inhaling an infective dose of anthrax bacteria, a man is likely to develop symptoms of pulmonary anthrax within 4 days. After a heavy dose, however, the incubation period may be less than a day.' The first symptoms are deceptively mild – usually just a normal cough. But the disease progresses rapidly. 'The victim develops a high fever, vomits; his head and joints ache and his breathing becomes increasingly laboured. He soon collapses and may die within 2 days or less' (Robinson *et al.* 1973). These symptoms are produced by toxins generated by the growth of bacteria in the patient's body.

Anthrax, which is not very contagious, is typically hard to diagnose until the terminal phase. This is a major problem because treatment, with antibiotics and immune sera, must be given soon after infection if it is to be effective. Relatively large doses of anthrax are needed to infect humans. 'Something of the order of 20,000 spores are needed to infect a man through his lungs.' Plague is seven times more virulent, and tularemia is a thousand times more virulent than anthrax. But anthrax has the largest death rate in untreated cases, 95 to 100 per cent, compared with 0 to 60 per cent for tularemia and 30 to 100 per cent for plague.

An example of the effectiveness of anthrax is the epidemic which broke out in Sverdlovsk, a city some 1,800 kilometres from Moscow, to the east of the Urals. More than a thousand people were said to have died from exposure to the bacteria.

What caused the outbreak is controversial. The American administration alleged that the research laboratories of a Soviet factory making biological weapons exploded on 3 April 1979. The laboratories were said to be near the hamlet of Kashino, about 30 kilometres from Sverdlovsk. The official Soviet explanation was that the deaths were caused by contaminated meat sold illegally. Anthrax is still common in parts of the former Soviet Union, and the epidemic may have originated in an accident in a vaccine plant.

Tularemia is caused by the bacterium *Francisella tularensis*, which can be cultured on a large scale. Early symptoms include chills, fever and respiratory difficulties. Chronic effects and debilitation are severe. Some strains, if untreated, have high mortality rates, although other strains are not very lethal.

An example of a typical incapacitating biological-warfare agent is Q (Queensland) fever, caused by the *Coxiella burnetti* rickettsia. Q fever is not directly transmitted from human to human but is exceptionally infectious (a single inhaled rickettsia may cause infection!). It is rarely fatal.

The rickettsia make good biological-warfare agents because they are easy to grow in tissue culture and can be stored for years without significant loss of viability. They are very hardy in aerosol form and can survive on surfaces for several weeks.

Q fever is similar to severe influenza and can be treated with antibiotics. If untreated, the illness may persist for up to three weeks and patients may be severely debilitated for several weeks afterwards.

The Venezuelan equine encephalomyelitis virus is rarely lethal in humans but very lethal in horses. It is relatively easy to grow. The virus is notorious for the wide range of hosts which harbour it.

Infection causes the sudden onset of influenza-type symptoms, including chills, vomiting, nausea, headache, aching limbs and debilitation. Most patients recover after about a week. The disease is not contagious but can be spread rapidly by mosquitoes. The virus is exceptionally virulent; a single virus may be enough to cause infection.

The anti-plant biological-warfare agent which causes the very destructive disease of rice called rice blast is the fungus *pyricularia oryzae*. Robinson *et al.* describe its production: 'It is easy to grow artificially. During growth it produces conidia, the minute seed-like spores through which it propagates itself. These constitute the potential biological-warfare agents. They are easily removed from the culture, and may be stored for long periods' (Robinson *et al.* 1973). As a biological weapon, the agent could be disseminated as a dust or sprayed as a liquid from aircraft spray tanks.

When a spore lands on a rice plant it will germinate and the fungus will penetrate the plant, eventually infecting all the plant tissue. 'Spore-bearing stalks will later grow out of the tissue to produce new spores that may be detached and scattered by the wind.' In this way, the disease is spread through the crop.

Diseased rice grains do not develop normally. The fungus also causes the stem to break so that grains in the head are lost. Rice blast can cause as much as 90 per cent of the crop to be lost.

Biological weapons

Research and development during the Second World War showed that it was possible to produce biological weapons capable of killing populations of people inhabiting a large area, rather than simply for sabotaging water and food supplies. Sabotage weapons normally use vectors, such as fleas or mosquitoes, to spread disease. But the most effective way of disseminating biological-warfare agents for mass killing is in a form suitable for inhalation or absorption through the skin or the eyes.

The most efficient biological weapon, therefore, releases its payload of liquid biological agent as a cloud of very small droplets; in other words, as an aerosol. An aerosol cloud will remain in the air for a significant time. As the cloud travels downwind, the biological agent will fall out of it slowly but steadily, contaminating the area under it.

Aerosol technologies have been well developed for a number of civilian applications, such as the agricultural dispersal of pesticides and paint-spraying. These can be readily modified for military use. Generally, the liquid agent is forced under pressure through a fine nozzle (hydraulic atomization) or the liquid is allowed to flow in a fine stream into a current of gas (air-blast atomization). Hydraulic atomization is used in, for example, bomblets; a small compressed-air cylinder provides the pressure.

But a simple way of dispersing a liquid biological-warfare agent is an aircraft spray tank. The agent is allowed to flow into, or just below, the slipstream of the aircraft, where it is converted into small drops of a suitable size.

Some biological-warfare agents are best dispersed in less rough ways. This can be achieved in powder form. In a typical bomblet, for example, a small cylinder of compressed air is arranged so that it directs a stream of air along the surface of the powder, blowing it out of the weapon uniformly through an exit slot.

Attitudes to biological warfare

Biological-warfare agents differ from chemical-warfare agents in that the military have never been much interested in biological warfare whereas they are more interested in chemical warfare. Biological agents tend to die quickly, unless in a precisely suitable environment. And their spread is extremely difficult to control. In fact, it is not well understood how epidemics spread. They come and go mysteriously and often die out inexplicably.

Another problem with biological weapons is that they may strike one's own troops as well as those of the enemy. Even if troops are vaccinated, there is always the danger that the disease will ultimately infect friendly civilian populations.

A final argument against the military use of biological agents is that they typically have relatively long incubation periods. Anthrax, for example, has an incubation period of up to four days; tularemia of up to five days; Q fever of up to twenty-one days; and rice blast of up to four days. The military are not keen on weapons that do not act almost immediately.

Although it is easier to mount a biological-warfare attack than to defend against one, protective measures, if adopted efficiently, can be effective enough to reduce considerably the military utility of biological weapons. One problem that the defender has, however, is that it is difficult to detect rapidly a biological-weapon attack; effective detectors that give both a selective and a rapid alarm are not readily available.

The disadvantage is somewhat offset by the delay before the effects of a biological attack show themselves. If an attack is suspected, medical measures can be taken in the incubation period to lessen considerably the severity of the effects of many diseases.

Protective measures include: the use of vaccines and other prophylactic methods of enhancing the body's natural physiological defences against disease; physical protection measures, like the provision of protective clothing, air-filtration and air-conditioned rooms; the destruction of biological agents before they can cause disease by, for example, the use of disinfectants; and medical measures to reduce the extent of the infection, particularly the use of antibiotics to treat diseases caused by bacteria and drugs to relieve the symptoms of diseases.

Vaccination is an obvious pre-attack precaution if an attack with biological weapons is feared. So far as the diseases caused by biological-warfare agents usually regarded as the most likely to be used are concerned, there are several vaccines available for anthrax, and a vaccine is available for each of tularemia, Q fever and Venezuelan equine encephalomyelitis. Vaccines are, however, not available for some potential biological-warfare agents, such as glanders.

Together, protective measures can make biological weapons militarily unattractive to the attacker. It must be emphasized, however, that unprotected populations, not organized to deal with a biological attack, with no, or a few, people trained in protective measures, and having no protective equipment or clothing, may well be decimated by biological weapons.

Large populations are, of course, difficult to protect. Treatment with antibiotics, for example, requires roughly 20 grams of antibiotic per person per dose. The maintenance of sufficient stocks to supply a large population would be an expensive and difficult logistic problem.

11

THE SPREAD OF BIOLOGICAL WEAPONS

One important similarity between biological and chemical weapons is that small nations could produce them relatively easily and cheaply in amounts which may, in the region, be strategically significant. This is why biological (like chemical) weapons are said to be potential weapons of mass destruction for smaller countries – 'poor countries' atom bombs', so to speak. There is considerable current concern about the danger that such weapons may proliferate.

Biological weapons programmes

Before the Second World War

Before the Second World War, no country had acquired modern biological weapons in strategically significant quantities. Earlier interest in biological warfare was related to the use of pathogens for sabotage rather than for the mass killing of people. But, according to Robinson, Germany, the UK, France, Japan and possibly the USSR were 'taking official or semi-official notice of biological weapons' in the 1930s (Robinson 1971).

Of the prewar biological-weapons activities, the Japanese research programme, begun in 1934, was by far the most extensive, involving the development of offensive capabilities as well as defensive ones. The organisms investigated by the Japanese as potential biological-warfare agents included all types of gastrointestinal bacterial pathogens, plague, anthrax and glanders.

The Japanese developed aircraft bombs to disseminate biological-warfare agents. One type produced aerosols of plague and anthrax; another was a fragmentation weapon which killed animals and people through anthrax contamination of wounds produced by shrapnel. It is also alleged that the Japanese developed bombs to spread plague-infected fleas.

The Second World War

German, French and British biological-weapon research before the Second World War was primitive and haphazard, producing negligible results. During the Second World War, the fear that Germany and/or Japan might use biological weapons on a large scale stimulated the United States and the United Kingdom to undertake research on these weapons. In fact, German biological-weapon research was negligible until 1943, when a research establishment was set up at Posen. Attempts were then made to develop aircraft spray tanks to disseminate plague, cholera, yellow fever and typhus. The possibility of using insects to attack enemy crops – mainly the use of Colorado beetles to destroy potato crops – was investigated. This research was not very successful.

In spite of reports of German interest in biological warfare during the 1930s, the British took virtually no action apart from stockpiling insecticides in case crops were attacked with insects, such as the Colorado beetle. Even during the Second World War very little British research was done into biological weapons. The main activity was an investigation into ways of disseminating anthrax spores.

The main Allied biological-weapon programme during the Second World War was American. American research work began in August 1941 at Edgewood Arsenal (Robinson 1971). Four years later, it was employing 4,000 workers, military and civilian. No detailed information about the results of American biological-weapon research during the war has been published in the open literature. But Robinson claims that a wide range of biological agents were studied:

> Pathogens studied at Camp Detrick included the bacteria of anthrax, glanders, brucellosis, tularemia, melioidosis, and plague; the virus of psittacosis; the fungus of coccidioidomycosis; a variety of plant pathogens – such as rice blast, rice brown-spot disease, late blight of potato, and stem rust of cereals; animal and fowl pathogens such as rinder-pest virus, Newcastle disease virus and fowl plague virus.
>
> (Robinson 1971)

This list, which may not be complete, indicates the extent of the American programme during the Second World War, which was clearly the world's largest.

Virtually no public information is available on the types of biological weapon developed by the Americans during the Second World War. About all that is known is that tests were made on a cluster-bomb designed to disseminate a biological-warfare agent fluid as an aerosol.

By the end of the Second World War, the various national research programmes had demonstrated the feasibility of using biological weapons as weapons of mass destruction, but none had yet produced a militarily effective biological weapon. Experimental data indicated that widespread disease could be produced in humans, animals and crops, particularly by the use of aerosols. It was left to postwar military scientists to use these results to manufacture a wide range of operational biological weapons.

After the Second World War

During the 1950s and the 1960s, large resources were devoted to the research and development of biological weapons by the United States and, presumably, by the USSR. Biological weapons became firmly integrated into the superpowers' military arsenals and, along with chemical weapons, integrated into their military tactics. The Soviet Union gave no information about the development of its offensive biological capability, and did not even admit its existence, but it is probably safe to assume that it roughly followed that of the USA.

The American programmes after the Second World War had the advantage of exclusive use of the results of the research into biological weapons carried out by the Japanese during the war (these were obtained in return for promises that Japanese military officers would not be charged with war crimes for their research activities). The American programme was centred on the main US Army biological-weapons research and development establishment at Fort Detrick. According to Susan Wright, the research network extended to 'contractors in approximately 300 universities, research institutes and corporations' (Wright 1990).

An interesting feature of the American biological-weapons programme in the 1950s and 1960s is the enthusiasm shown by the Central Intelligence Agency for biological (as well as chemical) weaponry for clandestine operations. In the words of Susan Wright:

> The principal CIA operation, code-named MKULTRA, began in 1953, focusing on techniques for controlling human behavior. Over the next ten years, investigations were pursued secretly in over 86 universities and research institutions, often with ruthless insensitivity to ethical considerations. Hundreds of human subjects were involved in tests of hallucinogenic and other drugs, sometimes without their knowledge or consent.

In 1969, President Nixon announced that the USA 'shall renounce the use of lethal biological agents and weapons, and all other methods of biological warfare', and that the USA 'will confine its biological research to defensive measures such as immunization and safety measures'. Three years later, the Biological Weapons Convention, banning the development, production and stockpiling of biological and toxic weapons, came into force. As of 1 January 1991, 112 countries had ratified the Convention.

Other than the United States, no NATO country has admitted to having an offensive biological-warfare capability between 1945 and 1972, although there are suspicions that France may have done so (in 1972, a government bill made illegal any French development, manufacturing or stockpiling of biological or toxin weapons). Most major powers, however, probably conducted defensive biological-warfare research. Many still do.

Egypt announced early in 1972 that it had biological weapons. Later in the year it signed the Biological Weapons Convention. Little is known about Israel's interest in biological weapons. Similarly, virtually nothing is known about China's activities in biological warfare.

Before the Gulf War, Iraq was suspected of developing biological weapons. According to the 4 June issue of the American magazine *US News and World Report*, the Centers for Disease Control in Atlanta sent three shipments of the West Nile Fever virus to Iraq. Such agents could be used in a biological-weapons programme.

Inspectors from the United Nations Special Commission inspected Iraq's biological research activities at Salman Pak after the Gulf War. Iraq admitted performing research into biological-warfare agents, beginning in mid-1986. Research was undertaken on *Clostridium botulinum*, *Clostridium perfringens* and *Bacillus anthracis*, said to be for both defensive and offensive purposes (Sigmund and Sigmund, October 1991).

At Salman Pak, the inspectors found a capability to research, test and store biological-warfare agents. Fermentation, production, aerosol testing and storing existed, but there was no evidence that biological weapons were produced and there was no facility for filling weapons with biological-warfare agents. Iraq handed over biological materials, including brucellosis and tularemia, which could be developed as biological-warfare agents.

Iran is also said to be producing biological weapons. According to American intelligence sources, about twenty countries may be developing biological weapons and about ten have biological-weapons programmes. The countries were, however, not named.

Interest in biological weapons does seem to be reviving. Advances in biotechnology are stimulating such interest. And, as Rosenberg and Burck point out, the number of natural biological agents mentioned as possible biological-warfare agents has increased (Rosenberg and Burck 1990). The most lethal ones are 'Marburg, Lassa, Legionnaires' disease, and Ebola viruses'.

12

MILITARY GENETIC ENGINEERING

The difficulty of controlling the spread of disease, the unpredictability of effects, the risk of infecting friendly populations, relatively long incubation periods, and the possible efficiency of protective measures are disadvantages which make natural biological-warfare agents militarily unattractive. But man-made agents, produced by genetic engineering, may not have these disadvantages.

The capability of an agent to withstand such environmental factors as humidity and temperature determines its survivability during its dissemination and storage and, therefore, its suitability for use in biological weapons. Genetic engineering techniques could be used to change the physical characteristics of biological-warfare agents to make them more suitable for use in biological weapons.

The production of new biological-warfare agents

Scientists are slowly but surely moving towards an understanding of the fundamental processes of life. We are on the threshold of a new biotechnological age. Recombinant desoxyribonucleic acid (DNA) and ribonucleic acid (RNA) research and other biotechnologies are making available a range of new biological substances (Novick and Shulman 1990). They are also leading to the understanding of ways in which human, animal and plant life can be damaged or destroyed. Military scientists are busily monitoring each new biological substance for its potential as a man-made biological-warfare agent.

Military genetic engineering is not new. As long ago as 1962, the US Department of Defense described American research and development activities in military genetic engineering as follows:

> attempting to obtain combination, recombination, or transformation with intact viral particles and/or their nucleic acid fractions; studying population genetics which includes the development of methods for inducing mutations and selecting such populations;

99

studying genetic changes occurring in cells and viruses in 'chronically infected' tissue-culture systems; isolating and attempting to recombine RNA from different viruses into a 'new' virus; studying the genetic compatibility between bacterial species of interest to biological operations; attempting to isolate or adapt bacteria and viruses to growth at high temperatures to improve resistance to thermal and aerosol stresses; attempting to isolate mutants of bacteria which are inherently more resistant to aerosolisation effects than parent strains; and applying genetic techniques for isolating mutants of pathogens which may be used for live vaccine preparations.

The scope of military genetic research has, of course, expanded in the past three decades.

A new generation of extremely lethal biological weapons is likely to emerge. These new biological weapons, unlike the old ones, may be of considerable military interest. They could be extremely contagious, consistent in their effects, safe to handle, difficult for the enemy to identify, and impossible for the enemy to vaccinate against.

There is a real possibility not only that new biological weapons will be developed, but also that only very small amounts of a culture may be needed to produce large quantities of a biological weapon in a very short time. The 1972 Biological Weapon (BW) Convention allows the production of small amounts of biological-warfare agents in advance because it can be claimed that they are for defensive purposes. Genetic engineering, in other words, may well make the BW Convention redundant.

Are the military interested in taking advantage of loopholes in the Convention? Breakthroughs in biotechnology have given the scientists the capability to produce new biological agents, not found in nature, which do not have the disadvantages of natural agents that make the military uninterested in them. Whereas the military are not interested in natural viruses and bacteria, they may well become interested in man-made ones.

Scientists can now identify and isolate specific genes and manipulate their structures. New genetic structures can be created, and these can be reproduced. By discovering the disease-carrying genes of dangerous viruses, scientists can greatly increase their lethality. Also, the genes which determine the lethality of the bacteria that produce diseases like anthrax and plague can be identified. These genes can then be spliced into bacteria that are normally harmless. Deadly genes from anthrax, for example, could be added to the bacteria *Escherichia coli*, a very prolific bacteria found in the gut.

The new man-made deadly *E. coli* could be quickly produced in very large quantities. They would be particularly deadly because being familiar to the human body they would be unlikely to produce antibodies. People infected with them would, therefore, not fight the disease.

Genetic engineering will not only make it possible to develop new and militarily interesting biological-warfare agents but it will also make it possible to develop vaccines specifically for the man-made diseases produced. The vaccines could be used to protect the troops and the population of the user. But the enemy will not know which diseases will strike him and will, therefore, be unable to protect his troops and population against them.

Military genetic engineers will be trying to develop ideal biological-warfare agents. The US Army Biological Warfare manual lists the desirable characteristics of biological-warfare agents as follows. The agent should consistently produce a given effect – the death or disablement of humans or damage to plants. It should be manufacturable on a large scale. It should be stable under production, while in storage, in munitions, and during transportation. It should be capable of efficient dissemination and stable after dissemination.

In addition, the ideal agent would be such that it is easy to protect the using forces against it; it is difficult for enemy forces to detect it and protect themselves against it; it has a short and predictable incubation period; it has a short and predictable persistency if the contaminated area is to be promptly occupied by friendly troops; it can infect more than one type of target – for example, humans and animals – through more than one portal of entry; it can be disseminated by various means; and it produces the desired psychological effects.

Until now, the production of strategically significant quantities of biological-warfare agents has been a time-consuming and difficult task. But genetic engineering will change all that. It will make it possible to produce large quantities of military effective and very lethal biological weapons in a short time and in small facilities.

The military use of genetic engineering is summarized by Steven Rose, brain researcher and expert in biological weapons:

> It is a fair guess that the military have looked at how to produce vaccines against a variety of biological agents, so that there would be some mileage in tailoring organisms to make them more resistant to antibiotics or vaccines. The existence of viruses with highly variable surface antigens that can circumvent the immune system, such as the AIDS agent HIV which mutates rapidly, could help. Other manipulations of organisms could include genetic tailoring to produce bacteria and viruses that are more virulent, or even to take bacteria that hitherto have not caused diseases and to

101

insert into them a gene that does. Alternatively, researchers could modify the distinguishing characteristics of bacteria that pathologists use for diagnosing infections. Finally, genetic engineers could design organisms that are easier to produce or store.

(Rose 1987)

A more sinister possibility has been suggested by Robert Harris and Jeremy Paxman:

The possibility of direct interference with human genes through the use of synthetic viruses opens the possibility not merely of ethnic weapons (designed to exploit naturally occurring differences in vulnerability among selected racial groups), but of wars in which the outcome would be decided not on the battlefield but with the birth of a mutant next generation.

(Harris and Paxman 1982)

The possibility of developing 'ethnic' weapons, although regarded as 'improbable' by such experts as Richard Novick and Seth Shulman, cannot be discounted. It would first be necessary to identify 'a protein specific for a particular population group', develop 'an antibody against this protein', and then to connect 'this to a toxin by gene slicing'. The toxin would have to be 'activated only as a consequence of the reaction between the antibody and the targeted protein'. The development of such racist weapons are beyond genetic engineers today; they are potentially tomorrow's weapons.

Incidentally, genetic engineering could make chemical as well as biological warfare more effective, and therefore more likely. The current treatment for exposure to a nerve gas is an injection of atropine, which blocks the effects of excess acetylcholine. But this is an unsatisfactory treatment because atrophine is itself toxic. There is, therefore, some military interest in alternative detoxifying agents. Research is being done to isolate the acetylcholinesterase gene, which could then be inserted into E. coli bacteria that could then produce large amounts of the enzyme. This would make an excellent prophylactic material for the treatment of people exposed to nerve gas.

13

CAN THE GLOBAL ARMS TRADE BE CONTROLLED?

Since the Gulf War there has been much talk about controlling the arms trade, particularly to the Middle East. Regional arms control is a major element in the Bush administration's agenda for a new Middle East order. But it is generally implied that control should be applied to regions other than the Middle East.

History shows that arms control in a region can be negotiated only when countries in the region feel secure. Security is, in other words, a prerequisite for arms control. It is hard to see tensions in many Third World regions being reduced – almost certainly a prerequisite for arms control – without far-reaching social and economic reform.

In the Middle East, for example, a relatively long process of confidence-building is probably a necessity before arms control can be negotiated. Arms control in the Middle East, and other unstable regions, is, therefore, an issue for tomorrow rather than today. Nevertheless, the desirability of controlling the supply of conventional weapons, as well as the control of the technology needed for the manufacture of missiles and weapons of mass destruction, to the world's unstable regions is now under active discussion. Another pressure for control is the growing realization of the connection between the illegal arms trade, drug-trafficking and organized crime.

Current restrictions on the arms trade

Current restrictions on exploring weapons vary considerably from country to country; arms-exporting policies are often decided on the basis of individual deals. Sweden is an example of a country with very restrictive arms-export regulations. No sales are allowed to: countries engaged in armed conflict; countries implicated in an international conflict which could conceivably lead to armed conflict; countries in which civil wars are taking place; and countries which may use Swedish weapons to suppress human rights.

Few countries have such a restrictive policy. The USA and other

103

western countries base arms-export controls on foreign policy and arms-control policy but mainly on the former. Russian restrictions are based on foreign-policy considerations. None of these countries believes that restraining arms transfers is an important goal for its own sake.

Generally speaking, governments must approve of important arms exports. But some major arms exporters interpret arms-export regulations more liberally than others. The UK, Germany and France all state in principle that they will not export arms to combatants at war or for use for internal repression. None of them sticks rigidly to its principles, but Germany and the UK implement restrictions significantly more stringently than France. France is, in fact, currently relaxing its regulations on arms exports.

In the USA, Congress must approve of any arms exports of 'significant military equipment' valued at more than $14 million and $50 million for other weapons. Bahrain, Jordan, Kuwait, Oman, Qatar, Saudi Arabia and the United Arab Emirates are Middle East countries that have had one or more requests for approval of orders for weapons refused by Congress since 1986 (Anthony and Wulf 1990). But, since 1988, Congress has softened its attitude and approved a number of large arms sales to the Middle East. Although President Bush froze arms exports to the Middle East after the Gulf War, the measure did not last long, except for the embargo on transferring weapons to Iraq.

In fact, according to the US Congressional Research Service, the value of arms agreements with Third World countries for American weapons increased by $10,500 million in 1990 after declining somewhat between 1985 and 1989 (Congressional Research Service 1991). Nevertheless, there are serious moves to control the global arms trade.

The European Community is trying to make the control of arms exports an element of the Treaty on European Political Union. The CSCE is promoting the publication by its members of information about arms export and import policies. And some governments and financial institutions (such as the World Bank, the IMF and the United Nations Development programme) are considering linking economic assistance with arms-import policies. At the same time, a number of governments are tightening up their national export regulations.

Controlling the spread of ballistic missiles

An attempt has been made to control the spread of missile technology by the establishment in 1987 of the Missile Technology Control Regime (MTCR), set up by eight western industrialized countries – Canada, France, Germany, Italy, Japan, Spain, the UK and the USA – to ban exports of ballistic missiles and associated technologies. Nine other countries, most recently Sweden and Israel, have joined the regime, bringing the number of members to seventeen. Russia has announced that it plans to restrict its export of ballistic missiles and missile technology.

The MTCR has made it somewhat more difficult to export ballistic-missile technology in the short term. But that the MTCR has major weaknesses is shown by the fact that many Third World missile programmes are making progress. The MTCR does not have an agency to detect non-compliance or any means of enforcement. It is not comprehensive, with, for example, China not participating. And there have been serious disagreements among participants about the interpretation of the agreement. The MTCR is unlikely to control effectively the proliferation of ballistic missiles in the medium and long term.

Encouraging moves to defensive weaponry

Given the strength of the pressures in favour of 'business as usual', it is hard to be optimistic about the prospects for any significant reduction in the value of conventional weapons transferred abroad in the foreseeable future. The customers are as keen to buy as ever. And pressures on suppliers to sell are increasing as military budgets decrease.

If the trade in conventional weapons cannot be significantly controlled, what can be done to reduce the destabilizing effects in Third World regions of powerful armed forces? One possibility is to encourage the acquisition of defensive rather than offensive conventional weapons. This is an attractive proposition because it corresponds with today's military technological realities. It would, of course, considerably improve stability in a region, particularly the Middle East.

A policy of encouraging Third World countries to restructure their military forces to emphasize defence rather than offence implies restricting the export of conventional offensive-weapon systems. Specifically, this would mean controlling the export of:

battle tanks weighing more than 25 tonnes;
armoured combat vehicles weighing more than 10 tonnes;
combat aircraft with combat radii over 500 kilometres;
frigates and larger warships;
ballistic and cruise missiles with ranges over 80 kilometres;
very powerful conventional weapons, such as fuel-air explosives.

The export of the following weapon systems would not be restricted:

light tanks weighing less than 25 tonnes;
light armoured combat vehicles weighing less than 10 tonnes;

artillery, including multi-launch rocket systems, with ranges up to 40 kilometres;
mortars;
combat aircraft with combat radii less than 500 kilometres;
naval ships smaller than frigates;
anti-tank, anti-aircraft and anti-ship guns and missiles;
land and sea mines;
anti-tank and troop-carrying helicopters.

It is not realistic to expect the negotiation of more far-reaching arms-control and disarmament measures in the Third World before the establishment of a satisfactory security system. In the meantime, the chances of eventually achieving significant control of the arms trade will be enhanced if the NPT and the BW Convention are strengthened and if a comprehensive ban on chemical weapons is negotiated.

But to hope for any arms control may prove to be too optimistic. It will be long remembered that during the Gulf War the infrastructure of Iraq, a Third World country, was destroyed by the high-technology conventional weapons of the advanced countries. The worst legacy of the war may be that Third World countries (in the Middle East and elsewhere) will conclude that, since they cannot themselves acquire and operate comprehensive high-technology conventional arsenals, their security can only be assured by the acquisition of nuclear weapons, perceiving that without these weapons they will be unable to deter effectively a country armed with the most modern weapons from attacking their territory.

Secrecy in the arms business

Perceptions about military matters are often more important than facts, even in policy decisions. Perceptions rather than facts are inevitably created and enhanced by secrecy. For example, current attempts by politicians to introduce stricter cash controls on spending by Britain's Ministry of Defence are made extremely difficult, to say the least, by the culture of secrecy in which the defence bureaucracy operates.

The British Parliament has virtually no access to the Ministry of Defence – a serious impediment to debate in a democracy! Much more access could be given without in any way jeopardizing national security. An illustration of the absurdity of the secrecy culture is the recent refusal of a Ministry of Defence civil servant to give Parliament's Defence Committee the number of Phantom combat aircraft deployed in Germany even though this number is published in the Treaty on Conventional Forces in Europe. The Ministry seems anxious to keep the British public ignorant of information readily available to the Russians!

Arms and technology exports from the UK are regulated and controlled by the Department of Trade and Industry. So far as these exports are concerned, this ministry also operates in secrecy; almost all contracts are kept secret for 'commercial' reasons. As recently as April 1991, Alan Clark, a Defence minister, told Parliament that 'the practice of successive governments' is 'not to provide information about arms export as it relates to specific countries'. If there is to be any transparency in the arms trade, Whitehall and industry must stop operating in this culture of secrecy.

In the USA, the perceived success of Patriot surface-to-air missiles against Iraqi Scud surface-to-surface missiles during the Gulf War has given a considerable boost to theatre anti-ballistic missile systems. But insufficient information is available in the open literature about the characteristics of the Patriot when used as an anti-ballistic missile to enable its performance to be evaluated. We know, for example, that several Patriots in Saudi Arabia launched themselves spontaneously but we do not know why.

Nevertheless, conventional wisdom has it that the Patriot is a very effective anti-missile system. The anti-ballistic missile programmes which will benefit by Patriot's perceived success – which include improvements for the Patriot system, a new missile called ERINT (Extended Range Interceptor) and a joint American–Israeli programme to develop a high-altitude interceptor missile called Arrow – are expensive. The Pentagon is asking for $858 million in fiscal year 1992 for theatre missile defence systems, more than double the 1991 budget. And Raytheon, the company making the Patriot, is, of course, encouraging perceptions of battle-proven success in its remarkably successful attempts to sell Patriot abroad but keeping secret adverse information about the missile.

It is, of course, necessary for national security reasons to keep secret some details of weapons. And there are commercial reasons for some secrecy. Weapons manufacturers face a dilemma here because most of the details about the weapons they produce have to be given to potential customers – including foreign customers – for the weapons.

The secrecy culture ensures that secrecy goes far deeper than is necessary for national and commercial security. In many cases, secrecy is based more on a desire to keep information from the country's own citizens than from a hostile, or potentially hostile, power. In fact, a great deal of information about all aspects of weapons and the arms trade is published in trade journals. These are read only by a small elite of specialists and defence analysts, and the information rarely becomes available to the general public.

There are three standard sources for information about the global arms trade. Annual registers are published by SIPRI, by the US Arms Control and Disarmament Agency, and by the US Foreign Affairs and National Defence division of the Congressional Research Service. SIPRI's register includes deals in major weapons. The two American sources also include small arms and spare parts.

SIPRI's information comes only from open sources, particularly trade journals. The American sources are based on American intelligence estimates, so that the raw data cannot be evaluated by independent researchers. It is generally recognized that each of the three sources underestimates the value of transfers of weapons. And, by their nature, none of the sources is up to date.

If we are to have transparency in the global arms trade, each government must make public information about the arms exported by the weapons companies in its country. From this information – supplied to, say, the United Nations – an official register of arms deals could be prepared. This would be a significant threat to the secrecy culture and will, therefore, be energetically resisted by the defence bureaucracies.

The idea of a register of the arms trade is supported in principle by most of the main arms-exporting countries, including all five permanent members of the United Nations Security Council. But as Herbert Wulf and Ian Anthony put it: 'The successful establishment of such a register will not contribute in any material way to enhancing world security. Its primary importance lies in the precedent it will set and as a first stage in a process that can be deepened in the number of items reported and expanded to include future as well as past transfers' (Wulf and Anthony 1991).

14

THE FUTURE OF THE NUCLEAR ARSENALS

Nine countries – China, France, Israel, the UK, the USA, Belarus, Kazakhstan, the Ukraine and Russia – have nuclear weapons. At the beginning of 1991, their arsenals contained a total of nearly 50,000 nuclear weapons. The former Soviet Union had about 25,000 nuclear weapons, the USA had about 20,000, France had about 600, China had about 300, the UK had about 400, and Israel had about 150 nuclear weapons.

In September 1991, President Bush announced significant unilateral cuts in America's nuclear arsenal. In October 1991, President Gorbachev responded by announcing significant cuts in the Soviet nuclear arsenal. These unilateral cuts followed limits on strategic nuclear weapons already agreed by the USA and the USSR in the START Treaty, signed in mid-July 1991.

The START Treaty

The START Treaty limited Soviet and American strategic nuclear arsenals to a total of 6,000 'accountable' nuclear warheads. Of these, 4,900 can be carried by strategic missiles – land-based intercontinental ballistic missiles (ICBMs) and submarine-launched ballistic missiles (SLBMs). There is a sub-limit of 1,100 warheads carried by mobile ICBMs.

The remaining 1,100 accountable warheads can be carried on strategic bombers, as free-fall bombs, air-launched cruise missiles, and short-range attack missiles. Bomber-carried nuclear weapons are not directly accountable on a one-to-one basis but are counted by a complex formula. This allows strategic bombers to carry relatively large numbers of nuclear warheads, while keeping within the accountable limit of 1,100.

For example, a future American strategic bomber force of 75 B-2 bombers and 96 B-1B bombers (each carrying 16 nuclear bombs and short-range attack missiles) plus 95 B-52H bombers (each carrying 20 air-launched cruise missiles) would carry a total of 4,636 nuclear warheads on 266 delivery vehicles but would be within the 1,100 'accountable' warhead limit.

Together with the 4,900 nuclear warheads allowed on ballistic missiles the post-START American nuclear arsenal could contain a total of about 9,500 nuclear warheads. The pre-START (mid-1991) American strategic nuclear arsenal consisted of a total of 11,966 nuclear warheads, carried on 1,000 ICBMs, 608 SLBMs, and 268 strategic bombers. The ICBMs carried 2,450 warheads, the SLBMs carried 5,216 warheads and the bombers carried 4,300 warheads.

In mid-1991 the USA deployed three types of ICBM – Minuteman II, Minuteman III and MX – and three types of SLBM – Poseidon C3, Trident I and Trident II. Apart from the Minuteman II, all the ICBMs and SLBMs carry multiple, independently targetable re-entry vehicles (MIRVs). American B-52 G/H and B-1B strategic bombers carried free-fall nuclear bombs, short-range attack missiles and air-launched cruise missiles.

The pre-START Soviet strategic nuclear arsenal consisted of a total of 10,880 nuclear warheads, carried on 1,334 ICBMs, 914 SLBMs and 106 strategic bombers. The ICBMs carried 6,280 warheads, the SLBMs carried 3,626 warheads and the bombers carried 974 warheads.

In mid-1991 the Soviet Union deployed seven types of ICBMs – SS-11 Sego, SS-13 Savage, SS-17 Spanker, SS-18 Satan, SS-19 Stiletto, SS-24 Scalpel and SS-25 Sickle – and five types of SLBM – SS-N-6 Serb, SS-N-8 Sawfly, SS-N-18 Stingray, SS-N-20 Sturgeon and SS-N-23 Skiff. Soviet Tu-95 Bear and Tu-160 Blackjet strategic bombers carried free-fall nuclear bombs and air-launched cruise missiles (International Institute for Strategic Studies 1991).

The START Treaty required the USA to reduce the number of its ballistic missile warheads by about 35 per cent and the Soviet Union to reduce the number of its ballistic missile warheads by about 48 per cent. In terms of strategic nuclear delivery systems (ICBMs, SLBMs and bombers), the USA was required to reduce its number by 19 per cent, and the Soviet Union was required to reduce its number by about 32 per cent. And the treaty required the Americans to reduce the number of nuclear warheads in their arsenal by 20 per cent or more. The Soviets were required to reduce the number of nuclear warheads in their arsenal by 34 per cent or more.

The START Treaty required the Soviet Union to reduce its 'heavy' SS-18 Stingray ICBMs, each carrying 10 MIRVS and regarded by the Americans as the most threatening strategic ballistic missile in the Soviet arsenal, by 50 per cent and the total ballistic missile throw-weight by 46 per cent (the treaty limited each side to a throw-weight of 3,600 tonnes). The Soviets had to reduce the number of their SS-

18s to 154 and agreed to eliminate twenty-two SS-18s a year for seven years.

Sea-launched cruise missiles (SLCMs) were not limited by the START Treaty, but each side made politically binding declarations about SLCMs carrying nuclear warheads with ranges over 600 kilometres. Both agreed not to deploy more than 880 of them. Pre-START, the USA had deployed 367 SLCMs and the USSR had deployed 100 SLCMs.

The tactical nuclear arsenals

The number of tactical nuclear weapons in the American nuclear arsenal in mid-1991 was about 8,000, and there were reported to be about 18,000 in the nuclear arsenal of the former Soviet Union. Of the American tactical nuclear weapons, about 4,000 were deployed in NATO Europe (including about 1,500 artillery shells, 662 Lance surface-to-surface missiles and 1,400 aircraft bombs) and about 2,500 in naval warships (including about 1,400 aircraft bombs, 325 Tomahawk sea-launched cruise missiles and 800 anti-submarine warfare bombs) (Norris *et al.* 1991).

Soviet tactical nuclear weapons included some 11,000 land-based systems (3,000 surface-to-air missiles, 3,000 surface-to-surface missiles, 3,000 aircraft bombs and 2,000 artillery shells) and about 3,000 tactical nuclear weapons carried in naval ships (about 1,400 aircraft bombs, 570 cruise missiles, 420 anti-submarine warfare weapons, 520 torpedoes and 200 surface-to-air missiles).

Unilateral reductions in the nuclear arsenals

The limits on strategic nuclear weapons set in the START Treaty were rapidly overtaken by the surprise announcement by President Bush of unilateral changes to be made to the American nuclear arsenal and the responding announcement of similar changes to the Soviet nuclear arsenal announced by President Gorbachev. The unilateral cuts in the American nuclear arsenal include the elimination of nuclear artillery and short-range surface-to-surface missiles. In addition, all tactical naval nuclear weapons are removed from warships and put into store. After the President's statement, NATO announced that the number of tactical aircraft nuclear bombs deployed in Europe would be halved (to about 700).

So far as American strategic nuclear weapons are concerned, strategic bombers are taken off alert and Minuteman II ICBMs removed from operational service. The President also wants the next START Treaty (START-2) to negotiate away all ICBMs equipped with multiple, independently targeted re-entry vehicles and suggested that the USA and Russia developed joint defences against ballistic-missile attack.

The impact of President Bush's initiative will be to destroy 3,050 tactical nuclear weapons (1,300 artillery shells, 850 Lance surface-to-surface missiles and 900 naval nuclear depth charges), and to withdraw and store 1,275 tactical nuclear weapons (350 SLCMs and 925 naval nuclear bombs). In addition, 2,690 strategic weapons will be taken off alert (including 450 ICBM warheads and 1,600 SLBM warheads). If ICBMs with multiple warheads are banned, another 1,500 warheads will be removed, excluding the 500 which would probably have been removed under START. The Bush initiative leaves unaffected 3,840 Trident SLBMs (Arms Control Association, October 1991).

President Gorbachev's response to the Bush initiative matched the American unilateral cuts and also suggested deeper cuts. Soviet nuclear artillery and short-range surface-to-surface missiles were eliminated. Strategic bombers were taken off alert, 500 ICBMs and three strategic nuclear submarines carrying SLBMs were taken out of active service, and all mobile rail-based ICBMs put into store. All tactical naval nuclear weapons were removed from warships and put into store and nuclear surface-to-air missiles destroyed or stored.

Other Soviet unilateral moves included stopping the development of three new strategic ballistic missile systems and a one-year moratorium on nuclear-weapon tests. President Gorbachev wanted START-2 to cut strategic nuclear weapons by a further 50 per cent. He also suggested negotiations to remove all tactical nuclear weapons on aircraft (bombs and missiles) and the multilateral negotiation of a comprehensive nuclear test-ban treaty, and was prepared to discuss with the USA the development of joint defence against ballistic-missile attack.

The Gorbachev initiative could reduce the Russian tactical nuclear arsenal by 10,000 land-based weapons (artillery shells, surface-to-surface missiles, nuclear mines and surface-to-air missiles), and 2,000 sea-based warheads. Some of these weapons would be destroyed and some put into storage. Gorbachev also proposed to remove, on a bilateral basis, nuclear bombs and missiles from tactical aircraft. In addition, Russian strategic warheads would be reduced unilaterally to 5,000 – 1,000 fewer than the 6,000 accountable warheads allowed under START (Arms Control Association 1991).

Other nuclear-weapon powers

Deep cuts in Russian and American nuclear arsenals will have ramifications for the other nuclear-weapon powers. As the Russian and American nuclear arsenals are reduced, those of China, France and the UK will become relatively more significant. Sooner or later, there will have to be negotiations about the future size and quality of all the arsenals. In the meantime, China, France and the UK intend to modernize their nuclear weapons (Norris *et al.* 1991).

The current British strategic nuclear force consists of four Polaris strategic nuclear submarines, each carrying sixteen SLBMs. Each SLBM carries three multiple re-entry vehicles, for a total of 192 nuclear warheads. In addition, the British have about 200 tactical nuclear weapons – about 175 land-based aircraft bombs and 75 naval nuclear depth bombs.

The British have announced reductions in the number of nuclear bombs deployed on tactical aircraft and the removal of naval nuclear weapons from all warships. But they plan to replace their Polaris submarines with four new Vanguard-class strategic nuclear submarines, each carrying sixteen American Trident SLBMs. Each SLBM may carry eight warheads, for a total of 512 nuclear warheads, a considerable increase in the size of the British strategic nuclear arsenal. The British are also considering a new tactical air-to-surface missile, to be developed in collaboration with France or the USA but with a British-designed nuclear warhead, to replace obsolete free-fall bombs on aircraft.

French strategic nuclear forces consist of five strategic nuclear submarines, each carrying 16 SLBMs, for a total of 400 nuclear warheads. In addition, the French have 18 land-based strategic missiles, each carrying one warhead and 18 nuclear weapons (air-to-surface missiles) carried on Mirage IV-P strategic bombers. Tactical nuclear weapons include about 75 land-based aircraft bombs, 40 Pluton surface-to-surface missile-launchers, and about 24 naval air-to-surface missiles.

French plans to modernize their nuclear forces have yet to be finalized. It is probable that land-based strategic ballistic missiles will be withdrawn. The Mirage IV-P bomber may be replaced with the Raphael D/M. The Pluton tactical missiles will be phased out and some replaced with a new surface-to-surface missile, the Hades.

Early next century the French strategic forces could contain 960 warheads on SLBMs and British strategic nuclear forces could contain 512 warheads on SLBMs, for a total of nearly 1,500 strategic warheads (BASIC, November 1991). The combined British and French nuclear arsenals could contain a total of about 2,000 tactical and strategic nuclear warheads by this time.

China has 8 ICBMs and 60 intermediate-range ballistic missiles, each equipped with one nuclear warhead. One strategic nuclear submarine carries 12 SLBMs, each with one warhead. China has up to 120 medium-range bombers, each carrying one or two nuclear bombs. China may be modernizing its ICBMs, making them solid-fuelled and equipped with MIRVs, and may be developing a more modern strategic nuclear submarine and a new bomber.

Israel's nuclear weapons are deliverable by aircraft and Jericho-II surface-to-surface missiles. The 1,500-kilometre-range Jericho missile is being further developed.

Conclusions

There is no doubt that the far-reaching nuclear disarmament now envisaged is an extraordinary and very welcome development, unbelievable only a short while ago. But many of the nuclear weapons removed from the arsenals by the Bush–Gorbachev initiatives are obsolete and would have been eliminated anyway. If all the proposals are carried through, the Russian and American nuclear arsenals will be reduced from a mid-1991 total of about 45,000 operationally deployed warheads to less than 6,000 operationally deployed warheads, an extraordinary amount of nuclear disarmament, reducing the strategic nuclear arsenals to levels far closer to a minimum nuclear deterrent. It is, however, unlikely that such deep cuts will be achieved before the year 2000. But the fact that the process is underway considerably improves world security.

There were significant differences in the Gorbachev and Bush announcements. The Americans were anxious to remove the threat of Soviet heavy accurate land-based ICBMs fitted with MIRVs. The Soviets were anxious to stop the modernization of American nuclear warheads and the development of new types of nuclear weapon by banning testing.

The Americans, however, intend to continue their modernization programme and, therefore, to continue testing. Although the Americans have abandoned plans to make their MX ICBMs rail-mobile, they intend to continue the development of the single-warhead Midgetman mobile ICBMs. The Midgetman is unlikely to be operational until 1997.

The American advantage in strategic nuclear submarines is likely to continue. The American strategic submarine fleet in the late 1990s may consist of 18 Trident submarines, each with 24 SLBMs, each SLBM carrying 8 warheads, for a total of 3,456 nuclear warheads. Ten Trident submarines are already operational or under construction.

The Russian strategic submarine fleet in the late 1990s may consist of 9 Delta III submarines (each with 16 SLBMs, each SLBM carrying 3 warheads), 10 Delta IV submarines (each with 16 SLBMs, each SLBM carrying 4 warheads), 6 Typhoon submarines (each with 20 SLBMs, each carrying 5 warheads), for a total of 1,672 warheads.

The concentration of strategic nuclear forces into submarines is a step in the right direction. For the time being, strategic nuclear submarines are relatively invulnerable so that an effective nuclear first strike will not be feasible, and nuclear war much less likely. A breakthrough in anti-submarine warfare technology might, however, make strategic nuclear submarines vulnerable and give the power that achieves it a strategic nuclear superiority.

The changes taking place in the Russian and American nuclear arsenals will make it difficult for the lesser nuclear-weapon powers to increase significantly the size of their nuclear arsenals, and one must, therefore, expect that some of the plans of these powers to do so will be modified. Research into and the development of nuclear weapons and their supporting technologies will almost certainly continue in all the declared nuclear-weapon powers. The quality of nuclear weapons will, therefore, continue to improve, activities that will be justified as 'essential modernization'.

15

THE INTERNATIONAL NUCLEAR NON-PROLIFERATION REGIME

Most governments believe that the further spread of nuclear weapons to countries that do not now have them, particularly to countries in unstable regions, is one of the most serious threats – if not *the* most serious threat – to global security and, therefore, to national security. There is considerably more concern about the spread of nuclear weapons than about the spread of chemical and biological weapons and ballistic missiles. This is justified because nuclear weapons have proved a much more effective deterrent and confer more regional status on their owner than chemical and biological ones. Moreover, chemical and biological weapons are militarily much less threatening than nuclear weapons. In the Gulf War, for example, Iraq's chemical-weapon arsenal and its ballistic missiles had little impact on the military tactics of the coalition forces.

Consequently, many countries are attempting to evolve national and international means of preventing or, at least, limiting nuclear-weapon proliferation and to strengthen the existing non-proliferation regime. Nevertheless, it is generally believed that the number of nuclear-weapon states will increase as time goes on.

The most important international non-proliferation instrument is the 1970 Nuclear Non-Proliferation Treaty (NPT). Other important nuclear non-proliferation measures include the establishment of zones free of nuclear weapons, the control of the export of nuclear facilities and materials, and the negotiation of a comprehensive test-ban treaty. But before discussing these it is useful to consider why countries want nuclear weapons in the first place.

Why countries go nuclear

The most important reasons why countries may acquire nuclear weapons are prestige, the need to solve real or perceived security threats, and domestic political motives. There is also likely to be a 'domino' effect in some regions, particularly unstable ones. If one country acquires nuclear weapons, a neighbouring country may feel obliged to do the same. Pakistan's nuclear-weapon programme was stimulated by the explosion by India of a nuclear device.

Countries like Israel have, or perceive that they have, security problems which they believe may be removed, or reduced, by the acquisition of nuclear weapons. India initiated a nuclear programme because of a security threat from a nuclear-armed China. And, in turn, Pakistan's nuclear-weapon programme is a reaction to India's nuclear capability. This is the way nuclear arms races develop.

Prestige is an important stimulant for the acquisition of nuclear weapons. The fact that all the permanent members of the United Nations Security Council are nuclear-weapon powers has a powerful symbolism, with obvious lessons for countries without nuclear weapons. Prestige (and pique at being forbidden access to American nuclear secrets by the 1946 McMahon Act, after contributing much to the Manhattan atomic-bomb project during the Second World War) was the main reason for Britain's nuclear-weapon programme. Prestige was also behind France's programme.

A nuclear-weapon force is still seen as an essential element in great-power status (and even more essential for superpower status). And smaller countries may see a nuclear-weapon force as a way of achieving leadership in their region.

Political leaders may want to develop nuclear weapons for internal political reasons – to satisfy the demands of the military, to boost domestic political prestige, or to distract the attention of the population from worsening internal social or economic problems. A country may acquire nuclear weapons for a mixture of these reasons. India very likely exploded its nuclear device in 1974 partly for domestic political reasons, partly to impress Pakistan, and partly to enhance its security against China.

After the end of the Second World War, the Americans claimed that they needed nuclear weapons to counter a perceived threat from considerably superior Soviet conventional forces. The argument was that the Soviets would not attack western Europe with their conventional weapons if they knew that their cities would, in retaliation, be destroyed with nuclear weapons.

Apologists for nuclear weapons usually argue that nuclear weapons have deterred war – and, therefore, kept the peace – in Europe for forty-odd years. Some take this argument further and claim that, if nuclear weapons increase security in Europe, they can perform the same function in other regions, such as the Middle East. There is little doubt that the behaviour of the declared nuclear-weapon powers stimulates other countries to acquire nuclear weapons. These powers are continually improving the quality of their nuclear weapons and are continuously developing technologies to support these weapons. By their behaviour they show that they believe that nuclear weapons have great political and military value.

They cannot, then, be surprised when other countries follow their example and acquire a nuclear-weapon capability of their own. It is simply unconvincing to argue that nuclear weapons are good for some countries but not for others. There is no reason for stating that nuclear weapons deter war in Europe but will not deter war in other regions.

Recent developments in the international non-proliferation regime

The international non-proliferation regime has recently been strengthened by the accession to the NPT of France, one of two declared nuclear-weapon powers which kept out of the treaty for many years. China, the other nuclear non-ratifier, has stated that it will join the treaty. China has been a bitter critic of the NPT, describing it as a plot against Third World countries. When China joins, Israel will be the only known significant nuclear-weapon power outside the treaty.

The NPT has also been strengthened by the recent accession of South Africa, a near-nuclear-weapon power. Tanzania, Zambia and Zimbabwe have also recently acceded to the treaty, creating a nuclear-weapon-free zone in southern Africa.

Argentina and Brazil, parties to the Latin American nuclear-weapon-free zone but not to the NPT, signed, in March 1991, a joint agreement under which they will submit their nuclear facilities to international inspections by the International Atomic Energy Agency (IAEA). Argentina and Brazil have significant civilian nuclear-power programmes and are near-nuclear-weapon powers.

As part of the Gulf War cease-fire agreement, the IAEA has the task of dismantling Iraq's nuclear-weapon capability. These developments have brought within the international non-proliferation regime a significant fraction of the known so-called 'threshold' nuclear countries – those with a capability to produce nuclear weapons or on the verge of such a capability. Now that South Africa is a party to the NPT, Argentina and Brazil are under IAEA safeguards, and Iraq is having its nuclear-weapon capability dismantled, the three countries remaining outside the regime which have nuclear weapons or a proven capability to produce them rapidly are India, Pakistan and Israel.

North Korea and Iran are suspected of having ambitions to become nuclear-weapon powers, even though they are parties to the NPT. North Korea has been a party to the NPT since 1985 and has initialled a draft agreement to submit its nuclear facilities to IAEA safeguards. Algeria is also suspected of having nuclear ambitions and, like North

Korea, is receiving assistance from China in acquiring nuclear technology.

Another important factor improving the chances of limiting the spread of nuclear weapons is the slowing down of the spread of peaceful nuclear technology, particularly nuclear-power reactors for the generation of electricity. As has been described, a major problem with nuclear reactors is that they produce plutonium as an inevitable by-product of the production of power.

That plutonium can be used as an exceedingly powerful explosive is the central threat of the nuclear age. The more countries that have access to plutonium, the greater is this potential threat. The complete fission of 1 kilogram of plutonium-239 would produce an explosion equivalent to that of 18,000,000 kilograms (18,000 tons or 18 kilotons) of TNT. Modern nuclear fission weapons have efficiencies approaching 40 per cent, giving explosive yields of 7 kilotons or so per kilogram of plutonium present.

The future of the nuclear industry

Clearly, the future spread of nuclear weapons is linked to the future of the civil nuclear industry. It is, therefore, important to analyse the future prospects for the nuclear industry. Between President Eisenhower's Atoms for Peace programme in the mid-1950s and the early 1980s, the nuclear industry was riding high. The oil-price increase in 1973 was a particular boost for it. A number of important countries – like France and Japan – became intent on reducing their dependence on oil imports by installing nuclear-power reactors. Another boost was the concern over the contribution to the greenhouse effect, and hence to global warming, from the atmospheric pollution produced by the burning of fossil fuels in power stations. Nuclear electricity was (and still is) promoted as being environmentally friendly.

During the 1980s, however, the nuclear-power industry suffered a series of shocks. The first was the realization that nuclear electricity was relatively very expensive. So uneconomic, in fact, that the British government was unable to include nuclear power in its electricity-privatization programme.

And in 1986 came the Chernobyl nuclear accident. Reactor safety then became a second major challenge to the nuclear-power industry. Safety and economics are, of course, intimately linked. The incorporation of expensive reactor-safety measures inevitably increases the cost of nuclear electricity. The difficulty of finding a politically and publicly acceptable solution to the problem of the disposal of high-level radioactive waste and concern about the health effects of low-level radiation

119

added to doubts about the wisdom of investing in nuclear-power programmes.

In 1970 the world's nuclear-power reactors were generating a total of about 20 giga-watts of electricity (1 giga-watt of electricity, or GWe, is 1,000 million watts of electricity). Five years later, this total had about quadrupled, to 75 GWe in 1975. It took another fifteen years for the total to quadruple again. Today, the world's total nuclear generating capacity is 326 GWe, generated by 423 power reactors (International Atomic Energy Agency 1991).

Predictions in the mid-1970s of the rate of increase of global nuclear generating capacity were exceedingly optimistic. By 2000, it was typically said, the world's nuclear capacity would reach 4,000 GWe and over 10,000 GWe by 2015. These huge increases would be achieved by the installation of large nuclear breeder reactors, each generating 4 GWe or more (on average, each existing nuclear-power reactor generates 0.77 GWe).

We now know that in the year 2000 the world's nuclear generating capacity will, in fact, be less than 400 GWe. There are at present eighty-three nuclear-power reactors under construction. When completed, these will add 66 GWe to the world's nuclear capacity. In the meantime, some of the reactors now operating will be shut down.

Currently, twenty-five countries are operating nuclear-power reactors. The USA operates 112 nuclear-power reactors, generating 101 GWe, 31 per cent of the world total capacity. France is operating 56 nuclear-power reactors, generating 17 per cent of the world total; the Commonwealth of Independent States operates 45 reactors, generating 11 per cent of the world total; Japan has 41 reactors, generating 9 per cent of the world total; and Germany has 26 reactors, generating 7 per cent of the world total.

These five top nuclear countries account for 75 per cent of the world total nuclear generating capacity. The next five countries in rank order are Canada (20 power reactors), the UK (37), Sweden (12), South Korea (9) and Spain (9). Together they add another 16 per cent to the world's total generating capacity so that the top ten account for 91 per cent of the total. The other countries operating nuclear-power reactors are: Argentina (2); Belgium (7); Brazil (1), Bulgaria (5); Czechoslovakia (8); Finland (4); Hungary (4); India (7); Mexico (1); the Netherlands (2); Pakistan (1); South Africa (2); Switzerland (5); Taiwan (6); and Yugoslavia (1). Four other countries – China, Cuba, Iran and Romania – which now have no nuclear power are constructing power reactors.

Post-Chernobyl many of these countries are modifying their nuclear programmes. Argentina is constructing its third nuclear-power reactor but it may never be completed because of escalating construction costs. Brazil is building its second power reactor but has had second thoughts about its ambitious nuclear programme, the future of which is very uncertain. Mexico's experience with nuclear power has been discouraging mainly because of the huge cost of building its single power reactor, and the future of Mexico's nuclear programme is much in doubt.

East European countries except Romania bought nuclear-power reactors from the USSR. There is now considerable concern in these countries about the safety of these reactors and much public opposition to nuclear power. Bulgaria has five operating reactors generating 36 per cent of the country's electricity, and two more reactors are under construction. Technical problems and local opposition are embarrassing the new government.

Czechoslovakia plans to close its two nuclear-power stations and may greatly reduce its dependence on nuclear electricity. Hungary has no plans to expand its nuclear-power programme, and the future of its four operating power reactors is uncertain. Poland has placed a moratorium on nuclear power until 2000. All of the nuclear-power plants in what was the German Democratic Republic have been, or will soon be, closed down. Romania started constructing five Canadian-supplied nuclear reactors in 1974, but none has yet been completed. Yugoslavia plans to close its only nuclear plant by 1995 and has declared a moratorium on new plants until 2000.

The Austrian government has abandoned its only nuclear-power station at Zwentendorf. Belgium has decided to postpone indefinitely the construction of new nuclear-power reactors. France is constructing six new reactors but, for economic reasons and concern about safety, future plans are uncertain. The German nuclear programme is being constrained. The Kalkar fast-breeder reactor and the Wakersdorf reprocessing plant have been cancelled.

The Netherlands, Switzerland and the UK have declared moratoria on new nuclear capacity, and Finland may soon do so. In 1980, Sweden announced its decision to phase out nuclear power by 2010 even though nuclear power produces as much as 46 per cent of the nation's electricity.

In the USA, no nuclear plant has been brought into operation since 1974. Public opposition has considerably curtailed Canada's nuclear programme, and plans to build twelve new reactors have been shelved, although the construction of two power reactors continues. Public opposition has stopped construction of two reactors in Taiwan.

The post-Chernobyl situation in the Commonwealth of Independent States is unclear. *Glasnost* has allowed public opposition to nuclear power to make itself felt for the first time ever. The future of the fourteen nuclear-power reactors of the Chernobyl type is, not very surprisingly, under consideration. And the construction of some of the twenty-five new nuclear reactors has been cancelled. But the nuclear establishment remains very influential.

Japan and South Korea are the world's most enthusiastic countries so far as nuclear power is concerned. Japan has ten and South Korea has two nuclear-power reactors under construction.

Currently, five countries generate nearly a half or more of their electricity using nuclear power. These are: France (75 per cent), Belgium (60 per cent), Hungary (51 per cent), South Korea (49 per cent) and Sweden (46 per cent). Seven more countries – Switzerland, Spain, Bulgaria, Finland, Germany, Czechoslovakia and Japan – use nuclear power to supply at least a quarter of their electricity.

Countries that are very reliant on nuclear power may have problems if they decide, for one reason or another, to reduce this dependence significantly. Sweden, for example, has had to develop a new electricity plan, relying on energy efficiency and renewable energy sources such as biomass, to replace nuclear power as it is phased out.

The status of potential proliferators

The existing non-nuclear-weapon countries which could most easily and rapidly manufacture nuclear weapons are those with nuclear-power programmes (or a uranium-enrichment capability). These are Argentina, Belgium, Brazil, Bulgaria, Canada, Czechoslovakia, Finland, Germany, Hungary, India, Japan, Mexico, the Netherlands, Pakistan, South Africa, South Korea, Spain, Sweden, Switzerland, Taiwan and Yugoslavia. These countries have the capability to produce fissile material for nuclear weapons and the expertise to design and manufacture them. The only thing between them and a nuclear-weapon force is the political decision to acquire one. Cuba, Iran and Romania are constructing nuclear-power reactors.

Countries operating research reactors – used to produce radioactive isotopes for medical or industrial purposes, or for education purposes – of significant size have the expertise to design and manufacture nuclear weapons. About fifty-two countries operate 323 research reactors (International Atomic Energy Agency 1991). The group of scientists and engineers that operate and maintain them could be diverted to a military nuclear programme.

But research reactors do not normally produce plutonium at a sufficiently high rate to manufacture over a period of, say, a few years the twenty or so nuclear weapons needed by smaller powers for a significant nuclear force. If a country without nuclear-power reactors decided to acquire nuclear weapons, it would probably acquire, perhaps clandestinely, a plutonium-production reactor. Israel, for example, did so.

122

Large research reactors could be used to produce plutonium for a nuclear-weapon programme. Algeria and North Korea are suspected by some of having ambitions to produce nuclear weapons using plutonium produced in such reactors.

Alternatively, countries may decide to use enriched uranium as the fissile material for nuclear weapons and build a uranium-enrichment plant for the purpose. South Africa has a nuclear-weapon capability based on enriched uranium. Pakistan has also used the enriched-uranium route to nuclear weapons and, before the Gulf War, Iraq was in the process of doing so.

Of the twenty-four non-nuclear-weapon countries who have, or soon will have, the capability to produce fissile material for nuclear weapons from nuclear-power reactors and the technical expertise to manufacture them, and the similar number of other countries that have a significant group of trained and experienced nuclear scientists and engineers and, therefore, the technical capability to initiate a nuclear-weapon programme, most have taken the political decision not to acquire nuclear weapons.

Most of the potential nuclear proliferators are among the 142 parties to the NPT, genuinely committed to the treaty and presenting no proliferation problem. South Africa was until recently regarded as (in the words of Thomas W. Graham) one of the undeclared *de facto* nuclear-weapon powers. Having joined the NPT it is now one of this number and now presumably intends to dismantle its nuclear-weapon capability. The remaining three undeclared *de facto* nuclear-weapon powers – India, Israel and Pakistan – are likely to remain outside the NPT for the foreseeable future.

Four Third World countries – Argentina, Brazil, South Korea and Taiwan – have significant nuclear-power programmes and, therefore, the capability to produce fissile material for nuclear weapons, and the technical expertise to manufacture them in a short time. These near-nuclear-weapon states have been suspected for some time of having nuclear-weapon ambitions, but it is now generally agreed that none of them will take the political decision to produce nuclear weapons in the foreseeable future. The Argentinian–Brazilian mutual nuclear safeguards system has removed the two countries from the lists of suspects, and both Taiwan and South Korea are unlikely to risk the wrath of the USA by manufacturing nuclear weapons.

Some parties to the NPT are suspected of having ambitions of acquiring nuclear weapons; these would be prepared to violate the treaty or abrogate it at a convenient time and are, therefore, not genuine NPT parties. Pre-Gulf War Iraq was the most notorious of this group. Others are Iran, Libya and North Korea. Algeria, not a party to the NPT, is also suspected of having nuclear-weapon ambitions. These five potential proliferators are in the process of acquiring the technical capability and the fissile material to become *de facto* nuclear-weapon states.

In summary, then, there are, in addition to the eight declared nuclear-weapon powers – China, France, Russia, Kazakhstan, Belarus, the Ukraine, the UK and the USA – three *de facto* nuclear-weapon powers: India, Israel and Pakistan. Given their technical capabilities and security concerns, Algeria, Iran, Iraq (still), Libya and North Korea must be regarded as potential proliferators. The main near-nuclear-weapon powers in the Third World – Argentina, Brazil, South Africa, South Korea and Taiwan – are very unlikely to take the political decision to become nuclear-weapon powers in the foreseeable future.

The 1970 Nuclear Non-Proliferation Treaty

The NPT attempted to freeze the number of nuclear-weapon states at five: China, France, the UK the USA and the USSR. The treaty, which came into force in 1970, commits, in Article I, the nuclear-weapon parties (the USA, the USSR and the UK) not to transfer nuclear weapons and not to assist in their manufacture by the non-nuclear-weapon states. Article II pledges the non-nuclear-weapon states not to receive nuclear weapons or control over such weapons, and not to receive any assistance in the manufacture of nuclear weapons.

To verify compliance, the non-nuclear-weapon parties must, under Article III, sign agreements with the IAEA submitting all their nuclear activities to IAEA safeguards (safeguards on all nuclear facilities in a country are called full-scope safeguards). To encourage non-nuclear-weapon states to ratify the NPT, Article IV promises co-operation and assistance to non-nuclear-weapon states in their peaceful nuclear programmes. Article VI of the treaty obligates those nuclear-weapon powers that have ratified it to take significant steps towards halting and reversing the nuclear arms race and towards nuclear disarmament.

Of the 160 or so countries in the world, 145 have ratified the NPT. At first sight, the NPT seems a strong treaty. But it is significantly weakened by the absence from it of Israel, India, Pakistan, Brazil and Argentina. The treaty is also weakened by the behaviour of the declared nuclear-weapon powers.

The maintenance of large, albeit reduced, nuclear arsenals and the continuous modernization of their nuclear weapons show that these nuclear powers continue to believe that nuclear weapons have significant political and military value. They cannot, then, be surprised when other countries follow their example and acquire a nuclear-weapon capability of their own. It is simply unconvincing to argue that nuclear weapons are good for some countries but not for others.

The initiatives of Presidents Bush and Gorbachev to reduce considerably the nuclear arsenals of the USA and the former Soviet Union will go some way to satisfy non-nuclear-weapon parties that the nuclear-weapon parties are taking their obligations under Article VI seriously and will strengthen the NPT. The negotiation of a permanent and comprehensive ban on nuclear-weapon tests would further strengthen the treaty.

In 1995 a conference of the parties to the NPT will be held to decide whether or not the treaty should continue. Many parties are very keen that a comprehensive test ban should be negotiated. Some of them may decide that the NPT is not worth maintaining. This would be a serious blow to efforts to restrain the spread of nuclear weapons.

Increasing the credibility of IAEA safeguards

Crucial for the credibility of the NPT is the international safeguards system operated by the IAEA under Article III of the Treaty. The thirty-two-year-old International Atomic Energy Agency (IAEA) has two main roles. One is to promote the use of peaceful nuclear technology; the other is to administer an international nuclear safeguards system to control civilian nuclear technology, specifically by detecting any 'illegal' diversion of nuclear materials from peaceful nuclear programmes to military use, particularly for the manufacture of nuclear weapons.

The problem is that, as has been described, military and peaceful nuclear programmes are, for the most part, virtually identical. In fact, the initial research and development of the nuclear fuel cycle was funded from military budgets. And, even today, the evolution of peaceful nuclear programmes depends, to a large extent, on the continuing interest in many countries in acquiring the capability to fabricate nuclear weapons.

Given the relationship between military and civilian nuclear programmes, can a single agency effectively promote and safeguard nuclear technology at the same time? Many observers argue that it cannot. Two recent events dramatically bring home the point and provide strong evidence that the effectiveness of the OAEA is seriously jeopardized by its attempt to combine the promotion and the control of nuclear technology. One wonders whether the IAEA will eventually founder in schizophrenic paralysis!

One event is the publication by the IAEA of a report, *The Radiological Consequences in the USSR of the Chernobyl Accident: Assessment of Health and Environmental Effects and Evaluation of Protective Measures*, describing the results of a year-long study by the International Chernobyl Project. The report suggests that the effects of the Chernobyl accident on human health – including cancer deaths, other illnesses and genetic effects – will be very considerably less than experts generally predict.

The IAEA Chernobyl report caused a furore. The report has been severely criticized by experts as scientifically flawed and politically motivated – influenced by the pro-nuclear-power lobby. In one expert's opinion, the conclusions of the IAEA's International Chernobyl Project are 'tantamount to erasing the [Chernobyl] incident from history'. The publication of the Project's report has, in the eyes of many, seriously damaged the reputation of the IAEA.

The other event is the illegal development by Iraq of a programme to develop nuclear weapons while a party to the NPT and, therefore, subject to IAEA safeguards on all its nuclear materials. The extent of Iraq's nuclear-weapon programme was not known until after the Gulf War, when Iraq submitted details to the United Nations. Not very surprisingly, the failure of the IAEA to detect Iraq's nuclear-weapon activities has raised questions about the efficacy of NPT safeguards.

The IAEA Chernobyl report

According to the IAEA report, exposure to radiation released by the 1986 explosion of the Chernobyl nuclear-power reactor has not produced any measurable physical health effects on the local population. No significant thyroid abnormalities due to radiation from the Chernobyl accident were discovered; nor were significant haematological or other effects on the immune system; nor were significant increases in cancers, genetic effects, cataracts or any other of the illnesses generally attributed to exposure to ionizing radiation. The study concludes that the only health effects of the Chernobyl accident are psychological, such as stress – a startling conclusion, fiercely challenged by, for example, the Ukrainian health authorities.

That exposure to ionizing radiation can damage human health in a variety of ways is general knowledge; the only debate is about the extent of the damage, specifically about the value of the risk factors – such as the probability of the induction of cancer and genetic effects for a given exposure (the radiation dose). How, then, can the report by an authoritative international agency like the IAEA conclude that the nuclear accident has had no radiological effects on the health of the local population?

At first sight, the report appears authoritative. About 200 scientists from twenty-five countries contributed to it, implying that the study was an impartial international assessment of the consequences of the Chernobyl nuclear accident. But the study had serious limitations – serious enough to cause the evidence on which it is based to be described as so inadequate as to be of very limited, if any, use.

126

These limitations may explain the report's strange conclusions. But because of them the report should never have been published, particularly given the importance and the political sensitivity of the subject, and the importance of maintaining the credibility of the IAEA, given its role in safeguarding the NPT.

Although large areas in Belarus, Russia and the Ukraine were contaminated with radioactivity from Chernobyl, exposing many hundreds of thousands of people to significant doses of radiation, the independent field-studies carried out by the International Chernobyl Project were rushed through in two months – far too short a time for an adequate study. The areas covered by the study were among those designated by the Former Soviet government as contaminated by more than a given level of radioactivity (5 curies per square kilometre of caesium-137) (International Chernobyl Project 1991). The government-designated areas are believed to underestimate considerably the contaminated regions in the three republics. The study should have covered a much larger area.

The number of people in the area examined by the Project was too small for adequate statistical analysis (the sample contained only 1,700 people from the contaminated and control areas); there was no complete census of the health effects on people in contaminated and comparable uncontaminated areas; the areas in which people in the control groups lived may have been contaminated by the accident; and hot-spots, areas of exceptionally high contamination, were not investigated.

The Project relied almost entirely on data supplied by the former Soviet government – hardly an objective source. This dependence on official data is perhaps the most serious criticism of the IAEA's Project. The data supplied were, in any case, most unsatisfactory, supplied in the form of statistics in tabular form, mainly as averages with no error bands included. Very few raw data or detailed contamination maps were submitted. The report admits that these limitations made impossible an independent comprehensive assessment of environmental contamination and reliable estimates of the doses of radiation to which people had been exposed.

The report has been heavily criticized because it excluded over 600,000 workers – mainly soldiers and miners – drafted in to clean up the mess caused by the explosion of the Chernobyl reactor (the so-called liquidators), as well as people living within 30 kilometres of Chernobyl (the so-called exclusion zone) and people already evacuated or relocated. In other words, the people who received the largest doses of radiation were left out of the study. The study was confined to about 825,000 people living beyond the exclusion zone. It should be noted that several million people live in areas near Chernobyl where the level of radiation is above that recommended as the maximum permissible for populations.

The conclusions of the IAEA report should be judged by reference to the radiological consequences of the Chernobyl nuclear accident predicted by experts and those actually observed by health authorities in the contaminated regions. These predictions and observations seriously contradict the IAEA report.

There is certainly much controversy about the effects of exposure to radiation from the radioactivity released by the Chernobyl accident on human health. One would have thought that the IAEA would have wanted to make a serious scientific contribution to the debate. But, as mentioned above, the International Chernobyl Project chose to ignore, for example, the effects of radiation exposure on the liquidators, even though they were among the most dramatic. Ukrainian experts estimate that about 7,000 liquidators have died from radiation exposure since the Chernobyl accident.

Many of the liquidators were exposed to very high doses of radiation. According to official Soviet figures, two workers died in the explosion and twenty-nine fire-fighters died from radiation sickness within a few weeks after the accident. A hundred and thirty-seven liquidators were said to have been hospitalized, and more than 300 were said to have suffered from radiation sickness.

Given the very high exposures to radiation involved, the Ukrainians' figures are more believable than the official Soviet ones. The IAEA seems unwilling seriously to challenge official Soviet figures, however blatantly incorrect they are.

Exposure to radiation can induce genetic effects which may damage the offspring of exposed people for generations. Crucial data on possible genetic effects from Chernobyl radiation were ignored in the IAEA report because it was described as 'unreliable'. This is a serious omission because genetic damage resulting from exposure to radiation of a large population is the most worrying of all radiation damage. The most recent statistics from the Ministry of Health in Belorussia report an 18 per cent increase in birth defects since 1986.

The International Chernobyl Project was set up at the request of the Former Soviet government, an important member-state of the Agency. The IAEA may, therefore, have been unwilling to diverge far from, or criticize, the official Soviet line about the effects of the Chernobyl accident. A more cynical view is that the International Chernobyl Project is simply a cover-up for the nuclear industry. Greenpeace, for example, has this to say: 'The report clearly illustrates the collusion of the international community with the cover-up of Chernobyl by Soviet authorities.

IAEA safeguards and Iraq's nuclear-weapon programme

One of the main tasks of the IAEA is to 'administer safeguards designed to ensure that special fissionable and other materials, services, equipment, and information made available by the Agency or at its request or under its supervision or control are not used in such a way as to further any military purpose' (Article III.5 of the IAEA Statute). The objective of safeguards is the timely detection of the diversion of significant quantities of nuclear material from peaceful nuclear activities to the manufacture of nuclear weapons or other nuclear explosive devices and the deterrence of such diversion by the risk of early detection. The IAEA safeguards system includes the application of measures for materials accountancy, supplemented by containment and surveillance.

To verify compliance with the NPT, parties must, under Article III, sign agreements with the IAEA submitting *all* their nuclear materials to IAEA safeguards. IAEA safeguards begin to operate when an agreement is signed between the IAEA and the country owning the nuclear material under safeguards which gives the Agency the right to make *ad hoc* inspections, routine inspections and special inspections. Inspectors are sent to the country to verify information that the country must give to the Agency about the location, identity, quantity and composition of nuclear material subject to safeguards. Although IAEA safeguards are designed to *detect* the disappearance of nuclear material rather than *prevent* such a disappearance, many exporters rely on the IAEA to safeguard nuclear material produced in exported nuclear facilities.

But the adequacy of the IAEA safeguards system is questioned by some governments. The Israeli government is one. In this context, no less a person than the Director General of the IAEA, Hans Blix, is quoted. Blix said on 11 December 1981: 'The safeguards do not, of course, reveal what future intention the State may have. It may change its mind on the question of nuclear weapons and wish to produce them despite possible adherence to the NPT. Neither such adherence nor full-scope safeguards are full guarantees that the State will not one day make nuclear weapons.' Ten years later, Iraq proved the Director General's point.

The case of Iraq is important because it shows that a country intent on making nuclear weapons can establish a nuclear-weapon programme while a party to the NPT, taking advantage of its membership of the treaty to obtain assistance in acquiring nuclear technology. It is, therefore, worth examining in some detail.

United Nations Security Council Resolution 687, which ended the Gulf War, addressed the issue of Iraq's weapons of mass destruction and was, therefore, a counter-proliferation action. The Security Council effectively established procedures for the 'destruction, removal, or rendering harmless' of these weapons and called for the development of a regime which would ensure over the longer term that Iraq's capacity for manufacturing weapons of mass destruction would not be redeveloped.

So far as nuclear weapons are concerned, Iraq is required to 'unconditionally agree not to acquire or develop nuclear weapons or nuclear-weapon-usable material or any subsystems or components or any research, development, support or manufacturing facilities related to nuclear weapons. The IAEA was nominated to carry out 'urgent on-site inspection and the destruction, removal, or rendering harmless of these and then to develop a plan for the long-term monitoring and compliance by Iraq of its obligations under Resolution 687'.

In a series of inspections of Iraqi facilities, the IAEA discovered that Iraq had been pursuing three parallel programmes to enrich uranium – electromagnetic isotope separation (EMIS), gas-centrifuge enrichment and chemical enrichment – and has successfully reprocessed neutron-irradiated uranium oxide samples to separate plutonium from them (United Nations 1991). Documents found by IAEA inspectors show that Iraqi scientists were designing an implosion-type nuclear weapon (a programme code-named Petrochemical Three) and a surface-to-surface missile, presumably as a delivery system for their nuclear weapon.

Documents also show that the Iraqis have separated a few kilograms of lithium-6 and apparently planned to produce annually about 100 kilograms of lithium-6. Lithium-6 is used in thermonuclear weapons (H-bombs). Typically, about 8 kilograms are used in a thermonuclear weapon.

Of the uranium-enrichment methods, top priority was given to the EMIS project, using calutrons. In a calutron, a high-current beam (several hundred milliamps) of low-energy uranium ions are passed through a magnetic field of about 5,000 Gauss. The heavier uranium-238 ions bend in a larger radius than the lighter uranium-235 ions, and suitably placed graphite collectors capture the separated isotopes. Much detail of the design of calutrons is in the open literature. But the snag is that a large amount of electrical energy is needed to operate them.

Apparently, the Iraqis began working on their EMIS project in 1982 at the Tuwaitha Nuclear Research Centre, near Baghdad. Iraq has been a party to the Non-Proliferation Treaty since 1969 and IAEA inspectors have been visiting Tuwaitha regularly (about twice a year on average) for many years. But the inspectors failed to discover the uranium-enrichment (and reprocessing) activities going on there. In fact, the calutron programme only came to light when an Iraqi defector blew the whistle to the Americans in May 1991.

The first experimental calutron operated at Tuwaitha had a beam curvature radius of 40 centimetres and a 1 milliamp current. In addition, one 50-centimetre and three 100-centimetre calutrons were built and operated; and a 120-centimetre model was designed for operation at an establishment at Tarmiya. The highest enrichments obtained were reported to have been 17 per cent uranium-235 for gram quantities and 45 per cent for milligram quantities (weapons-grade uranium contains at least 90 per cent uranium-235).

The Iraqis built and operated eight 120-centimetre calutrons at Tarmiya; the reported initial operating dates were between 23 February and 10 September 1990. A second batch of seventeen calutrons was being installed when Tarmiya was bombed in January 1991, although it appears that their ion sources and collectors had yet to be produced. Another building was under construction at Tarmiya apparently to house twenty 60-centimetre calutrons.

In all, the Iraqis had produced only about 500 grams of enriched uranium from their calutrons. The IAEA inspectors estimate that full production at Tarmiya would have taken much longer. There were difficulties in getting graphite for the collectors, and there were major design and operational failures at the facility at Al Jesira, near Mosul, which produced the uranium tetrachloride feedstock for the calutrons.

When all forty-five calutrons were in operation at Tarmiya they might have produced about 15 kilograms of weapons-grade uranium a year, assuming a 55 per cent availability – a very optimistic assumption given that the average availability of the eight operating calutrons was only 15 per cent. The Iraqis would need at least 25 kilograms of weapons-grade uranium for one nuclear weapon.

Iraq's gas-centrifuge enrichment project took second place to the EMIS project. Apparently, the project got under way in 1987 at Tuwaitha with the testing of a centrifuge using an aluminium cylinder 7.6 centimetres in diameter, rotating on an oil-lubricated bearing. This primitive model was abandoned in favour of one using a magnetic-pivot bearing.

Two types of rotor were planned for the second model: a maraging-steel rotor (with end caps and baffles welded into place) and a carbon-composite rotor (with caps and baffles held in place with epoxy resin). But the Iraqis said that only two tests had been carried out with this type of centrifuge, both using carbon-composite rotors acquired from abroad. Rotor speeds of 60,000 revolutions per minute (456 metres per second wall speeds) were achieved.

The performance of a gas centrifuge is measured in Separative Work Units (SWUs). Only one of the two tests actually enriched uranium hexafluoride gas, and during it the Iraqis claimed to have achieved an enrichment rate of about 1.9 SWU/year but hoped to improve this to about 2.7 SWU/year. This is by no means an impressive performance; the Pakistanis, for example, are achieving about 5 SWU/year/centrifuge.

The Iraqis planned to mass-produce gas centrifuges using maraging-steel rotors, even though these are less efficient than carbon-composite ones, at a factory near An Walid, 20 kilometres south of Baghdad. Vacuum housings, molecular pumps, and caps, baffles and the maraging-steel rotors were to be produced at the plant. The Agency inspectors believe that about 600 centrifuges a year could have been produced from the machine tools available at the plant.

But no centrifuge had actually been produced at An Walid. The Iraqis were unable to produce good enough maraging steel for centrifuges; the technology for flow-forming and welding maraging steel had not been developed. Nevertheless, they planned to have a 500-centrifuge cascade in operation by 1996. Whether or not the Iraqis could have achieved this is very uncertain. Not only were there the difficulties about producing maraging steel, but the IAEA inspectors also judged that the Iraqi scientists were still at an 'early stage of understanding of centrifuge technology'.

About 5,000 SWUs of enrichment are needed to produce enough weapons-grade uranium for one nuclear weapon. Assuming optimistically that the Iraqis could have eventually achieved 5 SWU/year/centrifuge, they would have needed 1,000 centrifuges operating continuously to produce one nuclear weapon a year. With an availability of about 30 per cent – another optimistic assumption – they would have needed more than 3,000 centrifuges to produce one nuclear weapon a year – and they planned to have only 500 operating by 1996.

The third element of Iraq's uranium-enrichment programme – chemical enrichment – was still in the laboratory stage. Both the Japanese resin method and the French solvent method were tried; the former was soon abandoned as being too expensive.

Iraqi nuclear scientists are certainly capable of designing an efficient nuclear-fission weapon, with an explosive yield equivalent to that of about 20,000 tons of TNT, weighing 150 kilograms or less, and deliverable by surface-to-surface missile. But, on available evidence, they would have taken at least four or five years to produce enough weapons-grade uranium for one such weapon. The Iraqis may not have had a militarily significant nuclear force of, say, twenty nuclear weapons until well into the twenty-first century.

The discovery that Iraqi scientists have reprocessed plutonium (even if only in gram quantities) is intriguing. This may suggest that they intended to build a clandestine plutonium-production reactor. The Iraqis had acquired at least 3 tons of heavy water (which, they say, was lost during the bombing), and they have lots of uranium. The production of plutonium for nuclear weapons – in, for example, a heavy-water – or graphite-moderated natural-uranium-fuelled reactor – is a lot easier and quicker than producing enriched uranium.

That the IAEA failed to detect any of Iraq's nuclear-weapon activities, all conducted while Iraq was apparently fulfilling its obligations under the NPT, has inevitably raised questions about the effectiveness of the NPT verification regime, and, therefore, about the worth of the treaty itself.

Improving the credibility of international nuclear safeguards

The IAEA clearly needs to improve the credibility of its safeguards system to convince people that it can ensure that parties to the NPT do not use material in their nuclear facilities to make nuclear weapons. This can only be done if the Agency gets more support from its member states. In particular, it needs access to intelligence data, especially information from Russian and American reconnaissance satellites. But perhaps the most important move would be to remove from the Agency all activities designed to promote nuclear technology so that it can concentrate entirely on its nuclear-control function.

Although 113 countries are members of the IAEA, its budget is only about $160 million, supporting a staff of some 2,000 professional and support staff. Currently, the Agency has about 930 nuclear facilities under safeguards in about sixty countries, requiring about 10,500 person-days of inspection a year. By the year 2000, this is likely to increase to over 15,000 person-days of inspection a year. The safeguards budget is, however, only about $60 million a year – just over a third of the Agency's total budget.

If the IAEA safeguards system is to be made credible enough to strengthen the NPT, the Agency safeguards budget must be increased. The best way of achieving this would be to maintain the Agency's budget but to confine its activities to the implementation of international safeguards. A move in this direction would significantly improve the prospects that the 1995 conference to decide the future of the NPT will conclude that the treaty is worth maintaining for some time.

Some experts argue a consequence of Iraq's violation of its safeguards agreement with the IAEA and of its NPT obligations by not declaring its indigenous production of enriched uranium and plutonium, albeit in small quantities, will be the strengthening of the international safeguards system and, therefore, of the NPT.

John Simpson, for example, argues that the following developments may now occur:

> First, the Nuclear Suppliers Group will add electronic separation (calutron) equipment to the supplier guidelines, and make the development of new guidelines for dual-purpose technology a top priority. Second, it is possible that the Western states and the Soviet Union will enhance their intelligence exchanges on potential nuclear weapons activities in 'suspect' states and seek a permanent, institutional mechanism for providing such information to the IAEA in order to trigger its special inspection procedure. Third, there will be demands to supplement the IAEA's standard safeguards agreement to cover facilities as well as materials, thus making the system more intrusive. Fourth, a precedent will have been established for Security Council and IAEA handling of safeguards agreement violations.
>
> (Simpson, October 1991)

Simpson proposes that IAEA–NPT safeguards should be made more stringent by covering nuclear facilities as well as fissile materials; that the IAEA should have the power to make 'special inspections' of facilities that NPT parties have excluded from safeguards. Incidentally, some lawyers argue that the IAEA already has the power to inspect these facilities if it suspects that fissile material is being illegally produced at them.

There is no doubt that UN Security Council Resolutions, such as Resolution 687, passed after the defeat of Iraq, suggest that the Council is prepared to act against states that violate their NPT obligations. But it should be noted that it is one thing to coerce a defeated Iraq by preventing it continuing with its nuclear activities and quite another to penalize in peacetime other potential proliferators, even if they are suspected of engaging in a clandestine nuclear-weapon programme. It should also be noted that Resolution 687 denies Iraq's rights, under Article IV of the NPT, 'to develop research, production, and use of nuclear energy for peaceful purposes without discrimination'.

The United Nations plans to establish an unprecedented regime under which Iraq faces an indefinite period of United Nations surveillance and inspections to prevent the re-establishment of a nuclear- and chemical-and-biological-weapons programme. Inspections will include civilian as well as military establishments. The special commission set up to dismantle Iraq's arsenals of weapons of mass destruction and ballistic missiles with ranges over 150 kilometres will continue to monitor Iraq's activities.

Iraq will be prohibited from importing a comprehensive list of chemicals, other materials, and components which could be used to produce weapons of mass destruction or ballistic missiles. United Nations inspectors will have the right to travel anywhere in Iraq, inspect any site, facility, activity, material or other item, and take any documents they consider relevant. Their inspections must not be hindered in any way and may be unannounced.

Will the UN be prepared in the future to intervene to such an extent in the internal affairs of sovereign states, even to the extent of taking military action, to prevent proliferation? Will the special commission set up to deal with Iraq be given powers to deal with other proliferators? Perhaps more intrusive IAEA inspections will be evolved. But it is difficult to be optimistic about truly coercive international actions, other than diplomatic ones. It will, for one thing, be difficult to persuade Third World countries that any threat to their sovereignty is not a new imperialism.

Whatever happens, the actions against Iraq, including the bombing of its research reactors and the postwar dismantling of its nuclear-weapon programme, may be seen by other developing countries as making the international non-proliferation regime even more discriminatory than many Third World countries already believe it to be. The suspicion will be enhanced that the main aim of the declared nuclear-weapon powers (i.e., the permanent members of the Security Council) is to maintain their monopoly on nuclear weapons. It will be hard to dispel these suspicions if these powers fail to persuade Israel to give up its nuclear weapons.

The fact has to be faced that any country with a significant nuclear-energy programme could, in time, produce nuclear weapons if it took the political decision to do so. The international proliferation regime, relying on the NPT and nuclear export controls, can slow down proliferation. And military action, perhaps under United Nations command, could destroy or deter a nuclear-weapons programme.

But the only effective way of preventing proliferation in the longer term is to persuade potential proliferators that nuclear weapons are of no military or political use to them and that their security concerns can best be satisfied by other means. This will, to say the least, be difficult to achieve unless the declared nuclear-weapon powers – the five permanent members of the Security Council – show that they believe in the non-utility of nuclear weapons.

Israel's attitude to IAEA safeguards and the NPT

Israel's criticism of IAEA safeguards is typical, if a rather extreme example, of the attitude of those concerned about the effectiveness of the NPT to prevent the spread of nuclear weapons. Israel is an active member of the IAEA but has always been critical of the Agency for what it sees as the Agency's pro-Arab attitudes. Israel accepts IAEA safeguards on the small research reactor at Nahal Soreq, imported from the USA in the late 1950s. But Israel will not accept safeguards on its nuclear reactor and other facilities (including the fuel-fabrication plant, the reprocessing plant, and the uranium-enrichment facility) at the Dimona nuclear centre. Other Israeli nuclear facilities not under safeguards include its uranium-purification (UO2) and uranium-conversion (UF6) plants and the heavy-water plant at Rehovot.

Israel showed its attitude to the international non-proliferation regime when it bombed the Iraqi research reactor in June 1981 – even though Iraq had ratified the NPT and the reactor and its fuel were under IAEA safeguards. Israel said that Iraq would have used the reactor to produce weapons-grade fissionable material for nuclear weapons and that neither IAEA safeguards nor other international non-proliferation measures were reliable enough to satisfy Israel that its national security was being protected. Later events were to prove that Israel was correct in its belief that Iraq intended to manufacture nuclear weapons.

Israel puts forward several reasons for not ratifying the NPT. The NPT does not, it argues, inhibit local wars, and local wars have been endemic in the Middle East. Israel believes that the IAEA safeguards system used to verify compliance with the NPT is inadequate. The Libyan leader, Colonel Gaddafi, is often quoted as saying, on 22 June 1987: 'The Arabs must possess the atom bomb to defend themselves, until their numbers reach one thousand million and until they learn to desalinate water and until they liberate Palestine.' And, as Israelis point out, Libya is a party to the NPT. Syria and other Arab countries qualified their accession to the NPT by stating that their obligations under the NPT do not imply the recognition of Israel.

The abrogation clause in the NPT is a major concern to Israel. Under Article X of the treaty a party can at any time declare its withdrawal from the treaty with three months' notice if it decides that 'extraordinary events' have occurred which 'it regards as having jeopardized its supreme interests'. The NPT, it is argued, allows a party to manufacture the components of a nuclear weapon, notify the IAEA and the UN Security Council that it is withdrawing from the treaty, and then assemble its nuclear weapons.

Avi Beker, a political scientist at Bar-Ilan University in Ramat Gan, gives a good summary of Israel's attitude to the NPT:

The fact that a majority of the world's states have accepted the NPT may create a false sense of security. The NPT was helpful in enlisting those countries which had already accepted the political realities of international and regional order. The treaty cannot provide security in regions wherein certain countries are determined to change the political order by threatening the very existence of others. In such regions, a country's signature on the NPT cannot be regarded as conclusive proof of its nuclear innocence but, on the contrary, can be exploited as a strategy for the acquisition of nuclear arms. A system that is inadequate for controlling international transfers of nuclear equipment, materials, and technology generally is especially impotent in dealing with the Arab–Israeli conflict.

(Beker 1986)

16

THE ESTABLISHMENT OF ZONES FREE OF NUCLEAR WEAPONS

India, Pakistan, Israel and North Korea are countries in unstable regions which have nuclear weapons (Israel and probably Pakistan), or could very rapidly manufacture them (India, which exploded a nuclear device in 1974), or are suspected of developing them (North Korea). India, Pakistan and Israel are outside the NPT. North Korea has ratified the NPT but has not yet agreed to submit its nuclear facilities to IAEA safeguards. The best way of persuading Israel – and Pakistan? – to get rid of its nuclear weapons and preventing India and North Korea from acquiring them may be to establish nuclear-weapon-free zones in their regions.

Nuclear-weapon-free zones

A nuclear-weapon-free zone, in its pure form, is an area from which nuclear weapons are totally excluded. The area covered may be part of a country, a whole country or a number of countries in a region. Nuclear weapons would not be allowed in such a nuclear-weapon-free zone under any circumstances. For example, a nuclear-weapon power would not be allowed to land military aircraft carrying nuclear weapons in any country which is part of a nuclear-weapon-free zone.

A legal definition of a nuclear-weapon-free zone is given in a UN Resolution of 11 December 1975. It is a zone 'recognized as such by the UN General Assembly, which any group of states, in the free exercise of their sovereignty, has established by virtue of a treaty or convention whereby: (*a*) the statute of total absence of nuclear weapons to which the zone shall be subject, including the procedure for the delimitation of the zone, is defined; and (*b*) an international system of verification and control is established to guarantee compliance with the obligations derived from that statute'.

A nuclear-weapon-free zone would generally include the territories, waters and airspace of two or more neighbouring states. Initially, a zone may be a limited area and later extended to include more countries as they agree to join. An essential element of an effective zone is a system of verification to ensure that all the parties involved comply with their obligations under the treaty.

For the purposes of a nuclear-weapon-free zone, a nuclear weapon can be defined as follows (as it is in the Treaty of Tlatelolco). A nuclear weapon is any device which is capable of releasing nuclear energy in an uncontrolled way and which has characteristics that are appropriate for use for warlike purposes. An instrument that may be used for the transport or propulsion of the device is not included in the definition if it is separable from the device and not an indivisible part of it.

A nuclear weapon is, for arms-control purposes, legally not a nuclear weapon until the component containing the plutonium or enriched uranium is put into it. If this component is stored outside the weapon, it is not legally a nuclear weapon. This means that a country describing itself as not having nuclear weapons could have made all the components. It only becomes a nuclear-weapon power when it assembles the weapons. This could, of course, be done very quickly. This difficulty of legal definition, which seems inevitable, is a weakness of all treaties banning nuclear weapons from some environment.

It should be remembered that the NPT commits the non-nuclear-weapon parties not to receive nuclear weapons, not to manufacture or otherwise acquire nuclear weapons, and not to seek or receive any assistance in the manufacture of nuclear weapons. If a region contains a group of countries that have ratified the NPT, it need not be a nuclear-weapon-free zone. The NPT allows the deployment of nuclear weapons in a party to the Treaty provided that the weapons remain under the control of the nuclear-weapon state that owns them. But a nuclear-weapon-free zone does prohibit such deployment and is, therefore, a more comprehensive ban on nuclear weapons than the NPT.

Existing nuclear-weapon-free zones

Nuclear-weapon-free zones have been established in a number of uninhabited regions: the Antarctic (by the 1959 Antarctic Treaty), outer space (by the 1967 Outer Space Treaty), and the seabed and the ocean floor (the 1971 Seabed Treaty). These nuclear-weapon-free zones were relatively easy to negotiate because the military have virtually no interest in deploying nuclear weapons in the regions concerned, which are all uninhabited.

The only inhabited regions to be declared nuclear-weapon-free zones are Latin America and the South Pacific. These zones were set up by the treaties of Tlatelolco and Rarotonga. The 1968 Treaty of Tlatelolco prohibits the testing, use, manufacture, production or acquisition by any means, as well as the receipt, storage, installation, deployment and any form of possession of any nuclear weapons by Latin American countries. The 1986 Treaty of Rarotonga prohibits the manufacture or acquisition by other means of any nuclear explosive device, as well as possession or control over such a device by the parties anywhere inside or outside the South Pacific zone.

A nuclear-weapon-free zone in the Middle East

An element of President Bush's New World Order is the establishment of a nuclear-weapon-free zone in the Middle East. The negotiation of a treaty banning all weapons of mass destruction may, in practice, be the only way of removing nuclear, chemical and biological weapons from the Middle East.

Israel claims that it is prepared to sit down with the Arab states and negotiate a nuclear-weapon-free zone in the Middle East. Negotiations for such a zone, and the local mutual arrangements that would have to be included in it, Israeli officials argue, would help prevent the outbreak of local wars in the Middle East. It will be remembered that in Israel's view the NPT does nothing to inhibit local wars.

The Arab states are unwilling to sit down with Israel and negotiate a nuclear-weapon-free zone in the Middle East because it would imply the recognition of the State of Israel. Breaking this Arab–Israeli impasse is the first step towards the negotiation of such a zone.

Each year since 1974 the United Nations General Assembly has adopted a resolution entitled 'Nuclear-Weapon-Free Zone in the Region of the Middle East'. Originally, the resolution was proposed by Iran, later joined by Egypt. Israel, which had not been consulted beforehand about the resolution, as is the normal diplomatic practice, did not support it and abstained during the vote.

But, in a speech to the UN General Assembly on 30 September 1975, Israeli Foreign Minister Allon proposed that all the important states in the Middle East should hold consultations about a nuclear-weapon-free zone in the region. In his words: 'Israel supports the proposal for a Nuclear Free Zone in the Middle East and will be ready to enter into negotiations with all states concerned in order to attain this objective. By negotiations we mean a process of intergovernmental consultations similar to that which preceded the adoption of the Treaty of Tlatelolco and other international instruments of like character. We do not think that so grave a matter can be settled by correspondence through the Secretary General.'

The Allon speech represented a change of Israeli policy. Previously, Israel had insisted that any arms-control measure in the Middle East should include conventional weapons as well as weapons of mass

140

destruction. Allon surprisingly dropped this linkage. But he would have known, of course, that it was extremely unlikely that a nuclear-weapon-free zone in the Middle East would be negotiated. The Allon speech, however, considerably reduced American suspicions about Israel's nuclear-weapon plans.

Since the 1979 Iranian revolution, Egypt sponsors the UN resolution on a nuclear-weapon-free zone in the Middle East alone. And, since 1980, Israel no longer abstains, so that there is a General Assembly consensus and the resolution is adopted without a vote.

Typically, the UN resolution:

Urges all parties directly concerned to consider taking steps required for the implementation of the proposal to establish a nuclear-weapon-free zone in the region of the Middle East and, as a means of promoting this objective, invites them to adhere to the NPT; calls upon all countries of the region that have not done so, pending the establishment of the zone, to agree to place all their nuclear activities under IAEA safeguards; to declare their support for establishing such a zone, and depositing those declarations with the Security Council; and not to develop, produce, test or otherwise acquire nuclear weapons or permit the stationing on their territories, or territories under their control, of nuclear weapons or nuclear explosive devices.

In a nuclear-weapon-free zone in the Middle East, the countries concerned would commit themselves to use any nuclear facilities and material under their jurisdiction exclusively for peaceful purposes. They would agree not to produce, or to acquire in any way, or to test, nuclear weapons and to prohibit, on their territory, the storage, receipt, installation or deployment of any other country's nuclear weapons.

The crucial Israeli demand is that a nuclear-weapon-free zone in the Middle East should be *negotiated*. The proposal for a nuclear-weapon-free zone in the Middle East, spelled out in the UN resolution, does not require any negotiations between the Arab countries and Israel. What is required is that the countries concerned join the NPT; in the meantime, to place all their nuclear facilities under IAEA safeguards; and to prohibit other countries' stationing nuclear weapons on the territories of the countries in the zone.

In other words, the resolution requires those countries in the Middle East that have not ratified the NPT to do so unilaterally, adding only the prohibition of third countries deploying nuclear weapons in the Middle East. Israel is, of course, one country that would have to ratify the NPT. But a number of Arab countries would also have to do so.

The geographical limits of a nuclear-weapon-free zone in the Middle

East would, of course, be established by the countries concerned. The typical region may well include the area stretching from Libya in the west to Iran in the east, and from Syria in the north to Yemen in the south. Of these countries, Israel has not ratified the NPT, nor have the following Arab countries: Algeria, Mauritania, Oman and the United Arab Emirates. Several sea areas may be considered for inclusion, including the Persian Gulf, the Red Sea and north-western parts of the Indian Ocean. The proposed zone includes countries having coasts in these sea areas.

The NPT ratification process does not require any negotiation. The other requirements of the resolution could be done by declaration. When Israel voted in favour of the Egyptian draft UN resolution on a nuclear-weapon-free zone in the Middle East it reserved its position on the modalities, stating that the principle of regional negotiation must apply.

In 1980, Ambassador Arieh Eilan, Israel's representative to the UN First Committee on Disarmament, introduced a resolution calling on the countries in the Middle East, 'and non-nuclear-weapon states adjacent to the region', to convene a conference to negotiate, 'regardless of their political differences and without prejudice to any political and legal claim', a multilateral treaty setting up a nuclear-weapon-free zone in the region.

The Arab states unanimously rejected the Israeli resolution. The Arabs were not prepared to accept 'negotiated regional arrangements'. Commenting on this, Israeli scholar Avi Beker writes:

> This is an unfortunate reality of the Middle East. Arab states refuse to participate in a multinational, treaty-writing conference which would require the acceptance of Israel as a legitimate Mideast entity and might imply the beginning of formal interstate diplomacy. The Iraq statement went even further by referring to the 'Zionist entity' (a usual Iraqi practice) and in fact denying Israel's right to even be at the committee.
>
> (Beker 1986)

Given the power of the Arab vote at the UN, Israel withdrew its resolution.

When they ratified the NPT, some Arab countries added the qualification that their obligations under the NPT did not imply recognition of Israel. The Arab countries are, therefore, unwilling to imply recognition of Israel by sitting down with it to negotiate a treaty. And, of course, it is, at least partly, to achieve recognition that Israel wants a conference.

Israel's demand for strong nuclear safeguards

The Israelis believe that a non-proliferation arrangement for the Middle East must contain a control and verification system that is much stronger than that provided by the IAEA. IAEA safeguards may work in regions that are stable and in which there are no immediate conflicts, but more stringent safeguards are required in unstable and conflict-ridden regions like the Middle East. Moreover, the acts of negotiating such safeguards and accepting the mutual arrangements that they would require may well have a stabilizing influence.

Those that argue for strong verification provisions often point to the Treaty of Tlatelolco as a model. Thus, the Foreign Minister of Israel, speaking in the UN General Assembly on 1 October 1981, after saying that the NPT 'cannot effectively prevent' nuclear-weapon proliferation in the Middle East, went on: 'The only genuine way to remove the nuclear threat in the Middle East can be found in the establishment of a nuclear-weapon-free zone, freely and directly negotiated among the countries of the region and based on mutual assurances, on the pattern of the Tlatelolco Treaty for Latin America.'

The Tlatelolco Treaty sets up a special permanent body to ensure compliance called the Agency for the Prohibition of Nuclear Weapons in Latin America with headquarters in Mexico City. The council of this agency has the power to carry out special inspections.

When so requested 'by any Party which suspects that some activity prohibited by this Treaty has been carried out or is about to be carried out, either in the territory of any other Party or in any other place on such latter Party's behalf, the Council shall arrange for the special inspection'. The parties undertake 'to grant the inspectors carrying out such special inspections full and free access to all places and all information which may be necessary for the performance of their duties and which are directly and intimately connected with the suspicion of violation of this Treaty'. In addition to this special verification system, each party to the treaty must negotiate an agreement with the IAEA for the application of its safeguards to its nuclear activities.

Undoubtedly, the provision for inspection by challenge by a special local body, in addition to IAEA safeguards, makes for a verification system that is considerably stronger than that provided by the NPT. Although it is no more able to prevent the diversion of fissionable material from peaceful to military purposes than the ordinary IAEA safeguards system, it makes it easier to investigate in a timely way a diversion which has taken place. This is why some Israelis argue that a nuclear-weapon-free zone in the Middle East must contain a verification system similar to that provided by the Treaty of Tlatelolco – one that provides a reliable system of inspection by challenge.

Another feature of the Treaty of Tlatelolco which many Israelis find attractive is Additional Protocol II. This obligates the nuclear-weapon states to respect the statute of demilitarization of Latin America, not to contribute to acts involving violations of the treaty and not to use or threaten to use nuclear weapons against the parties to the treaty. The NPT does not include such a provision.

A nuclear-weapon-free zone in the Middle East would be an effective way of strengthening the non-proliferation regime. It is, however, difficult to be as optimistic as some Israelis that a nuclear-weapon-free zone in the Middle East modelled on the Treaty of Tlatelolco would significantly reduce the likelihood of the outbreak of local wars in the region.

The support of Israel for a nuclear-weapon-free zone, coming after the 1979 Egyptian–Israeli peace treaty, is a gesture of goodwill towards Egypt. But will Israel give up its nuclear weapons to join a nuclear-weapon-free zone? Many doubt that it will – at least, until a comprehensive peace between Israel and the main Arab states has been established. Moreover, Israel will almost certainly demand that all weapons of mass destruction – chemical and biological as well as nuclear – must be included in a treaty banning all such weapons from the region.

17

CONTROLLING THE EXPORT OF NUCLEAR FACILITIES AND MATERIALS

The realization that the existing international measures to hinder, or prevent, the spread of nuclear weapons to countries that do not now have them need bolstering has led the major exporters of nuclear technology to establish guidelines for nuclear exports and some countries to adopt unilaterally national policies to control the export of nuclear materials and facilities.

These additional measures usually apply to nuclear exports to countries that do not accept full-scope safeguards – safeguards equivalent to those required by the NPT. They are, therefore, mainly aimed at importers of nuclear materials and facilities that are not parties to the NPT.

The Nuclear Supplier Group

The seven major suppliers of nuclear materials and facilities – Canada, France, Germany, Japan, the UK, the USA and the former Soviet Union – started meeting in London during 1975 to discuss ways of making the nuclear market-place less chaotic. The original seven have been joined by another nineteen suppliers – Australia, Belgium, Bulgaria, Czechoslovakia, Denmark, Finland, Greece, Hungary, Ireland, Italy, Luxembourg, the Netherlands, Norway, Poland, Portugal, Romania, Spain, Sweden and Switzerland – and the group has become known as the 'Nuclear Supplier Group'.

The group has drawn up a list of materials, equipment and technology, the so-called 'trigger list', which, when exported to any non-nuclear-weapon state, would 'trigger' IAEA safeguards. It also adopted guidelines for nuclear transfers requiring that countries receiving items on the trigger list pledge not to use them for the construction of nuclear explosives. Importers should also agree to provide effective physical protection for the materials provided.

The guidelines set up by the Nuclear Supplier Group apply to facilities for reprocessing and uranium enrichment and also for the production of heavy water. They apply to technologies directly transferred by the supplier or derived from the transferred facilities. The required safeguards apply also to any facility of the same type as that imported which is built indigenously during an agreed period, of some twenty years.

The Nuclear Supplier Group guidelines are not a treaty; they are of the form of a gentleman's agreement. Each member gives an undertaking to the other members to act according to the club's guidelines when exporting nuclear material, equipment or technology. A weakness of the Nuclear Supplier Group is that it does not require importers of nuclear materials and facilities to adopt full-scope safeguards (i.e., safeguards on all its nuclear facilities rather than on just those imported), as the NPT does. And the group's guidelines have not prevented some importers of nuclear technology and facilities using them in nuclear-weapon programmes. The best-known example is the use by Iraq of a range of imported materials in its nuclear-weapon programme.

National non-proliferation measures

A number of countries have unilaterally evolved national policies to bolster the NPT regime. These policies usually relate to the conditions under which nuclear materials and facilities are exported to countries – such as Israel and Pakistan – that have not ratified the NPT and do not accept full-scope safeguards.

Countries such as Australia, Sweden, Canada and the USA will only export nuclear materials and facilities to countries other than declared nuclear-weapon countries (China, France, Russia, the UK and the USA) if the importers accept full-scope safeguards or NPT membership. These strict nuclear exporters are at a commercial disadvantage when competing against nuclear exporters that are less strict, particularly France, Italy and West Germany that require the application of safeguards to the exported items only.

The conditions under which the USA, for example, will co-operate with other countries in nuclear technology were laid down as long ago as 1954 in the US Atomic Energy Act. This specifies, in section 123, that non-nuclear-weapon states must permit IAEA inspection of all their nuclear facilities to ensure that no nuclear materials, technology or equipment are being used in the manufacture of nuclear explosive devices. Section 129 states that non-nuclear-weapon states must not be engaging in activities involving nuclear materials that could be used in a nuclear explosive unless the President determines that the country is taking steps to terminate such activities.

The US Nuclear Non-Proliferation Act of 1978 places statutory requirements on American nuclear exports. It requires full-scope safe-guards. The American government has taken a number of other mea-sures to prevent the spread of nuclear weapons. These typically take the form of restrictions on foreign aid.

The 1976 Symington Amendment, for example, prohibits American aid to any non-nuclear-weapon state that imports or exports equipment or technology for the enrichment of uranium unless that country accepts full-scope safeguards. The President may waive the ban if he certifies that he has received reliable assurances that the country concerned will not acquire nuclear weapons or assist others to do so and that the ban on aid would have a serious adverse effect on 'vital US interests'.

The Symington Amendment, authored by former Senator Stuart Symington, is attached as an amendment to the Foreign Assistance Act. Although provoked by the 1975 West German agreement to sell Brazil a whole range of nuclear facilities, including a uranium-enrich-ment plant, it was aimed at dissuading Pakistan from developing nuclear weapons.

The 1977 Glenn Amendment, introduced by Senator John Glenn, bans the provision of American aid to countries that import plutonium-reprocessing technology or equipment. A sub-section was added to the Amendment in 1981 prohibiting American aid to any non-nuclear-weapon state that receives, detonates or transfers a nuclear explosive device. The President can waive the Glenn Amendment by certifying that not providing aid to the country concerned would seriously jeop-ardize America's non-proliferation policy or national security interests. But he cannot waive the sub-section for more than thirty days unless Congress enacts a new law authorizing the waiver.

The 1985 Solarz Amendment, introduced by Congressman Steven Solarz, bans American aid to any country found by the President to have illegally exported or attempted to export material, equipment or technology that could significantly assist it in the manufacture of a nuclear explosive device, if the President finds that the export was intended to be used for this purpose. The President may waive this ban if he determines that banning American aid would seriously harm American non-proliferation efforts or jeopardize the common defence and security.

United States law, therefore, requires that it stop economic and military aid to Pakistan if Pakistan should announce that it has nuclear weapons or if the USA should determine that it has them. This prohib-ition does not, however, legally apply to Israel. But as Warren Donnelly points out: 'To continue US aid if Israel declared [that it possessed] nuclear weapons would be seen by some countries as evi-dence that US support for Israel outweighs US non-proliferation policy, and would weaken US efforts to keep Pakistan and India away from such weapons' (Donnelly 1991).

Clearly, there is a difference between American nuclear policy to Pakistan and that to Israel. The pressure, from Congress and the White House, on Pakistan to prevent her manufacturing and – even more so – testing nuclear weapons is considerable and high-profile. But no such visible pressure is put on Israel to stop its nuclear-weapon programme. This difference clearly reflects the special relationship between Israel and the USA. But it shows very clearly that the USA is prepared to modify its non-proliferation policy for the sake of other foreign considerations.

18

THE NEED FOR A COMPREHENSIVE NUCLEAR TEST-BAN TREATY

Arguments for and against a comprehensive nuclear test ban

A comprehensive nuclear test-ban treaty, banning all nuclear tests, including those conducted underground, is often described as today's most urgent nuclear arms-control measure. A comprehensive nuclear test-ban treaty would achieve four important objectives. First, because testing is essential for the development of new types of nuclear weapon, a total ban on testing would stop, or at least considerably slow down, the nuclear arms race by preventing the development of new types of nuclear weapon. The vast majority of nuclear tests are performed to develop new warheads (International Foundation for the Survival and Development of Humanity 1991).

Second, nuclear weapons are taken at random from the nuclear arsenal and exploded to check that they still work effectively. If testing is banned, the military leaders are likely, sooner or later, to lose enough confidence in the reliability of their nuclear weapons to be unwilling to use them in a sudden pre-emptive nuclear attack. This would move nuclear strategies back from today's nuclear war-fighting strategies to nuclear deterrence by mutual assured destruction – a strategy which does not require very accurate or reliable nuclear weapons. Going back to nuclear deterrence by mutual assured destruction would significantly reduce the risk of nuclear war, including accidental nuclear war.

Third, a comprehensive test-ban treaty would hinder the spread of nuclear weapons to new countries and would strengthen the Non-Proliferation Treaty. Finally, it would stop the contamination of many underground nuclear-test sites with huge amounts of radioactive isotopes each year.

Those who argue for the continued testing of nuclear weapons put forward the following main arguments. First, there is a need to develop new types of nuclear warhead to make 'deterrence more effective' or to make nuclear war more 'discriminate'. In particular, these new warheads would, it is said, enable military targets to be destroyed without killing so many civilians and with less destruction of property. New types of American nuclear weapons now being researched include earth-penetrating warheads and the so-called 'third generation' nuclear weapons (the first generation of nuclear weapons are ordinary weapon-fission weapons; the second generation are thermonuclear weapons).

Nuclear weapons of the first and second generation all produce energy in the form of blast, heat and radiation, released uniformly in all directions. Nuclear weapons of the third generation, however, do not release all their energy in all directions but are designed so that some of the energy released by the nuclear explosion is focused in just one direction. Because of this, third-generation nuclear weapons are usually called nuclear directed-energy weapons.

In a directed-energy weapon, the primary energy released by a nuclear explosion is converted into X-rays, visible light, microwaves or charged particles. The conversion is done in such a way that the new energy is released in a focused way, in one direction – as a beam of light, microwaves or charged particles. American scientists are researching into directed-energy weapons based on X-ray lasers (Project Excalibur), pellet weapons (Project Prometheus, a nuclear shotgun firing a large number of exceedingly high-speed, very small pellets), microwave weapons, and optical lasers. The main interest in these weapons is their potential use in anti-ballistic missile systems.

Earth-penetrating warheads are shaped so that they burrow several metres into the ground before exploding. They are then able to destroy hardened underground targets, such as missile silos or command posts, as effectively as ordinary nuclear weapons of much higher explosive yield (perhaps twice the yield).

Those who argue against the development of these new types of nuclear weapon point out that none of them would make nuclear war significantly less lethal for civilians or increase the effectiveness of mutual nuclear deterrence.

The second argument for continued nuclear-weapon testing is that it is necessary to check that nuclear warheads still operate as designed. Without testing, the argument goes, the military would, over a period of, say, ten years or so, lose confidence in the reliability of existing nuclear weapons.

Those who oppose testing point out that without testing the military are likely to lose confidence, sooner or later, in their nuclear weapons as *nuclear-war-fighting weapons*. Even with a minimum nuclear deterrent there would be a sufficient number of nuclear weapons to provide a *nuclear deterrent*, even if they were so unreliable that only one in two got through to their target. A comprehensive test ban would, therefore, be stabilizing because the military would become unwilling to risk a nuclear first strike.

The third pro-testing argument is the need to match nuclear warheads to new delivery systems. A new nuclear warhead is not developed for its own sake but is tailor-made to fit a new delivery system. This is, however, not an essential practice. There is now such a range of warheads available that new delivery systems could be designed to match an existing warhead. There is no reason why, for example, the US Midgetman ICBM, now under development, should not carry the warhead used on the existing MX ICBM.

The fourth pro-testing argument is the need to improve the safety of nuclear weapons and to increase the security of them against unauthorized use. The chemical explosive used in some types of nuclear warhead is insensitive high explosive (IHE) which is relatively safe against an accidental nuclear explosion resulting from the detonation of the chemical explosive as a result of a fire or an impact at a single point. By no means all the nuclear weapons in the arsenals contain IHE, and nuclear testing is said to be necessary if those that do not have IHE are to be provided with it.

American nuclear warheads, except those on SLBMs, are equipped with permissive-action links (PALs) which prevent their detonation unless a secret code is keyed into an electronic switch. Russian PALs are fitted on the missiles rather than on the warheads. Some types of Russian and American warhead have additional security systems in which sensors prevent nuclear explosions unless they experience the correct sequence of accelerations, decelerations, and atmospheric-pressure changes expected for a trajectory from launch to target. The most advanced PALs are so integrated into the nuclear design of warheads that they require testing.

The planning for a comprehensive test-ban treaty would have to take into account any need to provide nuclear warheads with IHE and sophisticated PALs. If it were decided to fit additional warheads with these safety and security measures, it should be done and tested before the ban came into force.

The vast majority of nuclear tests are performed to develop new types of nuclear warheads. In an average recent year, the USA, for example, conducted about fourteen tests, of which about eleven were for new warheads (about three of them for third-generation nuclear weapons), one or two for safety and security, and one or two for warhead reliability. If nuclear tests for reliability, safety and security are considered essential in the short term, an alternative to going straight to a comprehensive ban on nuclear tests may be to negotiate a treaty allowing a small number of tests, perhaps one or two per year, each limited to a low explosive yield, of, say, 10 kilotons – a so-called limited low-threshold test ban.

The nuclear testers

Five countries – China, France, the former Soviet Union, the UK and the USA – have regularly tested nuclear weapons. India tested one nuclear device, in 1974, and it is suspected that South Africa, perhaps in collaboration with Israel, tested a nuclear weapon over the Indian Ocean in 1979.

So far, nearly 2,000 nuclear tests have been conducted since the first test at Alamogordo in the New Mexico desert on 16 July 1945 (Ferm 1991). On average, almost one nuclear test has been performed each week for the past forty-six years.

About 518 of these nuclear tests have been in the atmosphere, under water, or in space. In 1963 the Partial Test-Ban Treaty was signed, banning tests in the atmosphere, under water, or in space. The United States, the Soviet Union and the United Kingdom joined the treaty and moved their nuclear tests underground. But France continued testing in the atmosphere until 1974 and China did so until 1980. Since 1980, all five nuclear-weapon powers have conducted their nuclear tests underground.

Recently, the rate of nuclear testing has sharply decreased. In the past five years, for example, nuclear weapons have been tested at an average rate of thirty-one a year. In the five years before that, the average rate was fifty-two a year. This decrease in nuclear testing is due mainly to the end of the Cold War and to economic constraints.

So far, about 1,400 nuclear weapons have been tested underground, in many places around the globe. Although, in the short term, these have much less dangerous effects on health and the environment than atmospheric tests, they nevertheless release huge quantities of radioactive isotopes underground, some with half-lives of tens of thousands of years. Over the decades, some of these radioactive materials will almost certainly escape into the groundwater and thence to the human environment.

Environmental and health effects

The 518 or so nuclear weapons exploded in the atmosphere have contaminated the whole globe with radioactive material, radioactivity which still persists and which will continue to do so for thousands of years. These explosions released into the atmosphere an amount of radioactive fission products equal to that released by about 22,000

Hiroshima bombs. Exposure to the radiation from this radioactivity damages the health of people, past, present and future.

Today, our food and water supplies are significantly contaminated with the long-lived radio-isotopes caesium-137, strontium-90 and plutonium-239, produced by nuclear weapons. It is estimated that the total amount of caesium-137 released by atmospheric nuclear tests is no less than about forty times that released by the Chernobyl nuclear accident, the amount of strontium-90 released is about twenty times more, and the amount of plutonium is about 200 times more than that released by Chernobyl (International Physicians for the Prevention of Nuclear War (1991).

Most of this radioactivity was released in the 1950s and the 1960s. But these radio-isotopes have long lives, so that about a half of the caesium-137 and strontium-90, and virtually all of the plutonium-239, is still in our environment. These, and other radio-isotopes, are ingested or inhaled into the body, and exposure to radiation from them can seriously, sometimes fatally, damage health. According to estimates, radioactive materials from atmospheric nuclear tests incorporated into people by the end of the 1990s will produce a staggering 430,000 extra cancer deaths, some of which have already occurred (International Physicians for the Prevention of Nuclear War 1991). It is estimated that, eventually, as many as 2.4 million people may die prematurely of cancer.

The Soviets last tested a nuclear weapon on 24 October 1990 at Novaya Zemla, in the Arctic; this was the only Soviet test in 1990. In earlier years the Soviets were testing, on average, about twenty-five nuclear weapons a year, mainly at Semipalatinsk in Kazakhstan. Since 1985 there has been a great deal of publicity about the health effects of nuclear testing at Semipalatinsk.

It turns out that many of the underground nuclear tests burst through the earth's surface, releasing radioactivity into the atmosphere. Consequently, 10,000 or more people living in the Semipalatinsk region have been exposed to significant doses of radiation. Serious damage to the health of these people has already been reported.

According to some estimates, the incidence of cancer amongst this group may have been increased by as much as 40 per cent or so. And a considerable increase in thyroid disease, particularly among children, has been reported. These revelations, a result of *glasnost*, have caused well-organized and widespread public protest. And this is a main reason why there are now very few Russian nuclear tests.

There has also been much criticism of France for conducting nuclear explosions in French Polynesia, at Moruroa and Fangataufa atolls. Considerable damage has been done to the coral reefs there by about 123 underground nuclear-weapon tests, and significant amounts of radioactivity have been released into the marine environment. Radioactivity from the French tests will continue to leak into the Polynesian environment for many decades.

The governments of all the nuclear-weapon powers have deliberately withheld details about their nuclear tests from the public. As this culture of secrecy is penetrated by persistent researchers, it is discovered that the health and environmental damage done by nuclear-weapon testing is considerably more than was previously thought. People living near the test sites, those who participated in the tests, as well as the general public, have been exposed to higher doses of radiation than was previously assumed.

But most worrying of all are the risks to future generations from nuclear-weapon testing. It is well known that exposure to radiation can induce genetic effects which may damage the offspring of exposed people for generations. The exposure of people worldwide to radiation from atmospheric testing will produce significant numbers of mutations. The risks to future generations from underground testing have not yet begun to be studied seriously.

Conclusions

A comprehensive test-ban treaty, banning all nuclear tests, is an important arms-control measure. Not only would it considerably increase world security, particularly by hindering the spread of nuclear weapons to countries which do not now have them, but also the damage being done by the five nuclear-weapon powers by their nuclear testing to other people's health and the health of unborn generations can no longer be morally justified.

A comprehensive test-ban treaty would significantly strengthen the NPT. Many Third World countries feel so strongly about the need for a comprehensive test-ban treaty that they arranged that a conference was held in 1991 to consider amendments to the 1963 Treaty Banning Nuclear Weapon Tests in the Atmosphere, in Outer Space and Under Water that would convert it into a comprehensive treaty banning all nuclear tests. Because of the opposition of the USA, the UK and some other developed countries, the amendment conference failed in its purpose but kept open the option of its resumption.

A comprehensive test-ban treaty would have to be verified, to ensure that the parties were fulfilling their obligations under it. The technologies and methods of verifying such a treaty are well established, although their effectiveness may be debated. The main method of detecting underground nuclear tests is to use an array of seismometers to measure the ground motion caused by the nuclear explosion.

Experiments show that, using an appropriate network within, for example, the former Soviet Union of about thirty seismic stations, Russian nuclear explosions with explosive yields down to a few kilotons could be detected and identified with a confidence greater than 90 per cent, even if efforts were made to hide them. Many would regard this performance as adequate for the verification of a nuclear test-ban treaty on the grounds that nuclear tests with explosive yields below a few kilotons are of little military significance.

A global network of seismic stations could be established to monitor nuclear explosions worldwide with high confidence. It should be noted that to develop a new type of nuclear weapon many nuclear tests are required so that the verification of a comprehensive test ban would not need to be perfect.

19

CONTROLLING BIOLOGICAL AND CHEMICAL WEAPONS

Biological weapons

The military, as has been described, is not very interested in biological weapons at the moment. But military interest in biological weapons may increase in the future. This change of attitude will come about because of advances in genetic engineering. Military genetic engineers are monitoring progress in biotechnology to see if any new man-made biological agents are useful in biological warfare. Eventually, they may develop new biological weapons which prove to be so militarily effective as to be deployed in the arsenals of many countries.

Because of the danger that genetic engineering will produce horrific new biological weapons and the danger that many countries will acquire biological weapons, it is very important that the Biological Weapon (BW) Convention be made as effective as possible.

The BW Convention, which entered into force on 26 March 1975, prohibits the development, production and stockpiling of biological and toxin weapons. The convention prohibits the acquisition by any means or the retention of microbial or other biological agents, or toxins whatever their origin or method of production, of types and in quantities that have no justification of prophylactic, protective or other peaceful purposes, as well as weapons, equipment or means of delivery designed to use such agents or toxins for hostile purposes or in armed conflict.

The BW Convention specifies that the destruction of the agents, toxins, weapons, equipment and means of delivery in the possession of the parties, or their diversion to peaceful purposes, was to be effected within nine months after the entry into force of the convention. It was the first treaty since the Second World War to have led to the actual destruction of weapons.

By mid-1991, 112 countries had joined the convention. On 3–27 September delegates met in Geneva to review the operation of the treaty. It was hoped that they would take this opportunity to strengthen it (Goldblat and Bernauer 1991).

There is a major loophole in the BW Convention. Development and production of biological weapons are banned but research into biological agents is not. The prohibitions in the treaty apply only to types and quantities of agent that have no justification for medical, protective or other peaceful purposes. The term 'protective' covers the development of protective masks and clothing, air and water filters, detection and warning devices, and decontamination equipment. The production of some amounts of biological-warfare agents continues. As does laboratory and possibly field testing, as well as relevant military training.

These activities can have far-reaching consequences. For example, British military scientists tested a biological weapon containing anthrax on Gruinard, a deserted island off Scotland, in 1942. The island has only recently been decontaminated enough for humans to visit it.

Research involving the use of biological-warfare agents is supposed to be only for defensive purposes. But preparations for defence are, at some stages, indistinguishable from offensive ones. The convention fails to define the quantities of biological-warfare agents that are 'justifiable' for defensive purposes. It is, therefore, impossible to judge whether or not the production of a certain amount of an agent is illegal.

An example of the sort of problem that can arise occurred in 1982 when the Americans accused the Soviets of violating the convention. The allegations, which have been repeated by the Americans ever since, were related to the outbreak of anthrax in Sverdlovsk, a city some 1,800 kilometres from Moscow, in 1979.

The Americans alleged that the anthrax came from research laboratories of a Soviet military factory illegally making biological weapons. According to Soviet physicians, sixty-four people died during the epidemic, which went on for several weeks. The official Soviet explanation was that the deaths resulted from the handling and consumption of contaminated meat sold illegally.

Even if the epidemic was caused by the accidental release of anthrax spores from a military laboratory, it would not be possible to show that the activity was illegal under the Biological Weapon Convention. The amounts of biological-warfare agents that can be produced legally are simply not defined in the convention.

Unfortunately, the delegates at the recent Review Conference did not close the research loophole. But they did agree that parties to the convention will declare whether any development, testing and production of specified biological agents are taking place on their territories, and the establishments in which these activities are being performed. This new openness will be a useful confidence-building measure.

Another weakness in the Biological Weapon Convention is that there are no provisions in it to verify that parties are fulfilling their obligations under the treaty. The Review Conference discussed the possibility of establishing a verification system. But all that could be achieved was agreement to set up a group of experts to look into the technical feasibility of verification. Further action on verification will have to wait until the next Review Conference in 1996.

The problem is that, in the meantime, considerable advances will almost certainly be made in genetic engineering. Sooner or later, a range of new man-made biological agents will emerge which do not have the disadvantages of natural agents.

The fact that the convention allows the production of relatively small amounts of biological-warfare agents for so-called defensive purposes is important because only very small amounts of a genetically engineered culture may be needed to produce very large quantities of a biological weapon in a very short time. Genetic engineering, in other words, may well make the Biological Weapon Convention redundant, unless military uses of any products of genetic engineering are unambiguously banned. This should be the main purpose of the next Review Conference.

Chemical weapons

The 1925 Geneva Protocol

The horror generated by the use of chemical weapons in the First World War had one positive result: the negotiation of the 1925 Geneva Protocol prohibiting the use of asphyxiating, poisonous or other gases and of bacteriological methods of warfare. As of 1 January 1991, 125 countries had ratified the protocol. Actually, all nations are, according to most international lawyers, bound by the protocol because a ban on the first use of chemical and biological weapons has become a well-established customary international law, binding both on parties and non-parties.

But the protocol has a number of weaknesses. It does not prohibit the development, production and stockpiling of chemical weapons. And many of the parties, including the USA and Russia, have reserved the right to use the weapons to retaliate in kind. Generally speaking, therefore, the protocol only bans the *first use* of chemical and biological weapons.

The protocol was seriously weakened by the use of chemical weapons in the Iran–Iraq War between 1983 and 1988 by Iraq and possibly by Iran. The fact that there was little international criticism of Iraq, the main culprit, for using chemical weapons has, of course, been noted by all countries. The lack of criticism is all the more serious because the use of chemical weapons by Iran and Iraq is without doubt a blatant violation of international law. Both nations are parties to the Geneva Protocol.

Because the combatants got away with their illegal use of chemical weapons, and because Iraq obtained a significant military advantage by chemical warfare, we must expect that many countries are now thinking about acquiring chemical weapons for their arsenals.

The Australia Group

Efforts to control the export of key precursors – the chemicals used to produce chemical-warfare agents – centre on the activities of the so-called Australia Group of countries: Australia, Belgium, Canada, Denmark, France, Germany, Greece, Ireland, Italy, Japan, Luxembourg, the Netherlands, New Zealand, Norway, Portugal, Spain, Switzerland, the United Kingdom and the United States. The group set up by the chemical-weapons precursor-export warning list which currently contains fifty substances.

The list is circulated by the governments of the Australia Group to their chemical industry advising it that caution should be used in the export of the chemicals because of their potential military use. Nine substances on the list form the 'core list' for which the countries in the group have introduced or are introducing export controls. A permit must be obtained before a core-list chemical is exported. Export controls are not export bans; they simply place certain conditions on exports.

Controlling the export of precursors is difficult because most of them have legitimate commercial uses for, for example, manufacturing pesticides. Also, if a country cannot obtain a specific precursor it can buy the chemicals from which the precursor is made and manufacture it.

For these reasons, and because the export of precursors is not banned, the Australia Group activities cannot do more than hinder the spread of chemical weapons. Countries like Iraq and Libya have developed their chemical-warfare capabilities by importing chemicals and technologies from members of the Australia Group.

A more effective way of controlling the spread of chemical weapons would be the negotiation of a comprehensive ban on chemical weapons, prohibiting the development, production and stockpiling of chemical weapons. The negotiation of such a convention has been going on without success for a number of years at the forty-nation Conference on Disarmament in Geneva.

For some time, two main obstacles to the negotiations were the American policy of reserving a right to retaliation with chemical weapons and the American insistence on retaining 2 per cent of its chemical-weapon stockpile until all countries having chemical weapons had joined the convention. In May 1991, President Bush announced that the USA would drop these requirements. The remaining obstacle to the conclusion of a treaty is the question of verification.

20

VERIFICATION TECHNOLOGIES

The purposes of verification are detecting violations, or possible violations, of a treaty, thereby providing early warning of any threat to the
state's security arising under a treaty regime; deterring violations of
an agreement by increasing the risk of detection and complicating any
attempts at evasion; acting as a domestic and international confidence-
building measure in the viability of an arms-control treaty; and providing data for the presentation of arms-control issues to the public
(Lyddon and Lingwood, June 1988).

The utility of any arms-control or disarmament treaty will depend
to a large extent on the effectiveness of its verification provisions.
Verification is, therefore, a crucial issue. It is also a highly technical
issue, often relying on sophisticated sensors on board satellites or
complex arrays of seismic monitoring stations.

Verifying a chemical-weapon treaty

Just how complex verification can become is shown by the proceedings
at the current negotiations at the forty-nation Conference on Disarmament in Geneva on a comprehensive ban on chemical weapons,
designed to prohibit the development, production, stockpiling, acquisition, retention or transfer of chemical weapons, including lethal and
incapacitating chemicals and their precursors. The verification of this
treaty will probably have to deal with: obligations to be checked by
systematic international on-site verification; the destruction of stockpiles of chemical weapons by continuous monitoring with on-site
instruments and the continuous presence on site of international
inspectors; and the destruction of chemical-weapon production facilities by monitoring with on-site instruments and periodic international
on-site inspections.

In addition, there may be provisions for some mandatory routine
international on-site inspections of the destruction of chemical-weapon
stocks; the verification of non-production at declared facilities; and

161

challenge inspections to deal with cases of suspected non-compliance which may not have been revealed by regular inspection of declared facilities. Any buildings, other than domestic habitations, may – in theory at least – be subject to inspection.

The verification procedures will require novel technical equipment, particularly for the continuous chemical analysis, by spectrometry and other methods, of effluents from various parts of chemical plants. The appropriate technologies exist, but suitable monitoring equipment is under development.

The verification requirements for a chemical-weapon treaty are comparable with, or more complex than, the safeguards procedures for verifying the provisions of the NPT, elaborated by the IAEA. Although confidence in these procedures has been shaken by Iraq's undetected violation of NPT safeguards, they have, over the past fifteen years or so, acquired considerable credibility with the parties to the NPT. The IAEA is a large agency, employing a large international staff, including some 200 professionally trained inspectors, and having an annual budget of $100 million. A global chemical-weapon treaty will probably require the establishment of another verification agency, comparable in size to the IAEA, to verify it.

National technical means

A number of arms-control treaties – including the Antarctic Treaty, the Partial Test-Ban Treaty, the SALT I and SALT II Treaties, the Threshold Test-Ban Treaty, the Intermediate Nuclear Forces Treaty and the START Treaty – contain an explicit prohibition of interference with 'national technical means', thereby legitimizing these techniques for collecting information about other countries' activities. National technical means are, and are likely to remain, the most important verification techniques.

The technologies used for arms-control verification are essentially the same as those used to gather military intelligence. These currently rely mainly on photographic cameras carried on board satellites; the monitoring of radio and radar communications generated by military activities, an activity called electronic intelligence (ELINT) and normally performed by electronic equipment carried on satellites; the collection of data by other satellite-borne sensors, particularly infra-red sensors; and the seismic monitoring of underground nuclear tests. Clearly, the family of sensors carried on satellites – including photographic cameras, television cameras, multi-spectral scanners, radiometers, microwave radars, gamma-ray detectors, X-ray detectors, and detectors of electronic and communications signals – are crucial in verification activities.

These national technical means are supplemented by information collected by: on-site inspections; espionage (the clandestine collection of information by human agents operating on the territory of other countries); and audits and accountancy to check the production of materials controlled by arms-control treaties. The START Treaty, for example, allows for nine types of on-site inspection: baseline data inspections, data update inspections; new facility inspections; suspect site inspections; re-entry vehicle inspections; post-exercise dispersal inspections; conversion or elimination inspections; close-out inspections; and formerly declared facility inspections (US Arms Control and Disarmament Agency 1991). But photographic reconnaissance satellites – like the American KH-11 (Keyhold) and the Russian Cosmos satellites – are today's intelligence work-horses and are likely to remain so for some time, although satellites carrying infra-red sensors also play an important role.

Photo-reconnaissance

There are two types of photo-reconnaissance satellite activities. One is to scan a large area of territory with a wide-angle low-resolution camera. If there is something suspicious on the photographs, it is investigated with a high-resolution ('close-look') camera. Some photo-reconnaissance satellites are devoted to just one activity, but current American KH-11 satellites carry both close-look and wide-angle cameras. These satellites typically have perigees of about 250 kilometres.

The resolution of the best high-resolution cameras used on reconnaissance satellites is a closely guarded secret. But, when the atmosphere is reasonably clear and the weather is fine, resolutions of 10 centimetres or less are probably achieved at orbital altitudes of about 250 kilometres (Krass 1985).

With a resolution of 10 centimetres, the following are among the objects that can be precisely identified and described in considerable detail on satellite photographs: bridges, radar sites, supply dumps, troop units, airfield facilities, rockets and artillery, aircraft, command and control headquarters, surface-to-surface and surface-to-air missile sites, surface ships, vehicles, land minefields, ports and harbours, coasts and landing beaches, railway yards and shops, roads, and surfaced submarines (*Reconnaissance Handy Book* 1980). Photographs taken with high-resolution cameras show impressive detail and are extremely useful for verification purposes. In the words of William Colby, the late director of the Central Intelligence Agency: 'You can see the tanks, you see the artillery, but you may not quite see the insignia on the fellow's uniform' (Colby 1979).

Nevertheless, photo-reconnaissance is limited by cloud cover and poor light. And, of course, objects that are underground, underwater, inside buildings, or otherwise hidden, cannot be photographed with light. These difficulties can to some extent be overcome by using infra-red and radar images.

Infra-red reconnaissance

The earth's atmosphere is transparent to infra-red radiation. Infra-red of some frequencies can make developable some types of photographic film and is called photographic infra-red. Although photographic infra-red can penetrate haze to a useful extent, cloud cover still seriously limits its use in satellite photography. And so does darkness. But its use does considerably improve contrasts.

All objects in nature emit, absorb or reflect radiation in a unique way. Objects can, therefore, be identified by detection and measurement of their characteristic radiations. Camouflaged objects, for example, create a spectral response different from their surroundings, and differences in photographic infra-red reflectance can improve photographic contrasts enough to show up camouflaged objects.

Infra-red can also be used to detect radiation emitted by warm and hot objects with infra-red detectors. Although these can be made very sensitive, infra-red images from satellite-borne detectors have much worse resolutions than photographic ones, mainly because of larger atmospheric diffraction effects. In fact, satellite infra-red resolutions are typically a hundred times poorer than those for visible light. Nevertheless, infra-red imagery has important potential uses in verification. It could, for example, be used to detect the movement of vehicles at night, and camouflaged or otherwise hidden activities.

Satellite radar

High-resolution images of objects on the ground can also be obtained by synthetic aperture radars (SARs) carried on satellites. A ground-based radar usually has a large antenna to obtain a good resolution. But to be practicable in outer space a radar must have a relatively small antenna. An SAR uses a cunning method to get a good resolution with a relatively small antenna.

It uses the motion of the antenna relative to the ground to increase the effective length of the antenna. As the antenna, equivalent to the aperture of a camera, moves with the satellite in its orbit, the radar signals reflected back from objects on the ground are received by the antenna and recorded; they are later analysed by a data-processing system. The maximum length of the synthetic aperture is the length of the satellite path along which the moving antenna receives the reflected radar signals from a given object; the effective length of the antenna is thereby increased.

The resolution of an SAR is typically some ten times worse than that from optical photographs, but SAR pictures can be obtained through the thickest clouds at any time, day or night. Another advantage of SAR, compared with optical and infra-red sensors, is that its resolution is independent of the distance between the antenna and the distance of the object of interest. SAR satellites can, therefore, be operated in high enough orbits to give them long lives.

CCD technology

Some reconnaissance satellites use charged-couple devices (CCDs), semi-conductors sensitive to light, in linear arrays of detectors (Jasani and Barnaby 1984). The arrays are used in place of a film. The CCDs store an electric charge in the pixels (picture elements) that is proportional to the intensity of the light. After exposure, the charge at each pixel is read directly by computers and transmitted directly to a ground station. The use of films, and their time-consuming development, is thereby eliminated.

The CCD is an important new technological development that makes easier the collection of intelligence in real time, an extremely useful capability for some verification purposes. The resolution of the images obtained with an array of CCDs is reportedly as good as photographic films.

Verifying conventional force reductions

The Conventional Armed Forces in Europe (CFE) Treaty, reducing conventional weapons in Europe, includes very large numbers of weapons – armoured vehicles, aircraft, helicopters and artillery guns – which are relatively small and very mobile. The treaty stipulates that the countries of the old Warsaw Pact alliance, on one side, and NATO countries, on the other side, are each limited to 20,000 tanks, 30,000 armoured combat vehicles, 20,000 artillery pieces, 6,800 combat aircraft and 2,000 attack helicopters.

The verification of the CFE Treaty is mainly by intrusive inspection. Each country (twenty-two involved) is obliged to give the others detailed information annually about the size and whereabouts of its forces in Europe. Each country can check this information by sending teams of inspectors to other countries. Inspections are to check that no more weapons are being held at military site than have been declared as being held there. Surprise visits, called challenge inspections, can be made to check that weapons are not held anywhere else, including non-military sites. Russia alone has to be ready to receive about 200 inspections a year.

In addition to the normal national technical means, there are a number of technological systems which can be used to verify treaties controlling conventional arms, whether in Europe or in any other region. Flying military aircraft can be monitored by existing systems, such as Airborne Warning And Control System (AWACS) aircraft.

Systems such as the Joint Surveillance Target Attack Radar System (JSTARS) can detect, identify and track moving columns of tanks, armoured personnel-carriers and other vehicles. JSTARS is an airborne system using side-looking radars able to observe objects within a circular area of a 150-kilometre radius.

An individual land vehicle, such as a tank or an armoured combat vehicle, can be provided with a token containing biological material from an individual animal or human which could be genetically unique and forgery-proof. In addition, the token could be equipped with a hologram, extremely difficult to replicate and which could be checked on the spot. Tokens could also be provided with integrated circuits broadcasting a signal on interrogation or sending telemetry signals with a tamper-resistant code.

Storage areas for armaments can be monitored by infra-red sensors, able to monitor the dimensions of vehicles, and video sensors; buried sensors, particularly seismic sensors; and X-ray sensors to monitor exits (Dean 1989). The verification of the Intermediate-range Nuclear Forces (INF) Treaty already includes this sort of storage-area monitoring.

Buried strain-sensitive cables can be used to register movements of vehicles crossing it: passive infra-red scanners to distinguish between people and vehicles, count numbers of persons or vehicles passing, and register direction and speed; and miniature seismic intrusion detectors can be used to detect vehicles at distances of up to 500 metres.

Verification may also involve detecting intruders into monitored areas. Active-beam alarms systems, in which intruders break the beam, use infra-red and microwave beams, but low-level laser beams may become the favoured system because the beam is finer and less affected by adverse weather conditions. For detecting intruders, however, microwave systems have the advantage of relatively wide coverage area, which makes it difficult to bridge the system. Microwave beams, which are very effective detectors, generally have longer ranges than infra-red or laser beams – up to 200 metres compared with 100 metres.

Fence detection systems typically use acoustic cable in which a treated coaxial cable attached to the perimeter fence acts as a microphone. A signal is generated when an intruder tries to get over the fence or cuts the cable. A more sensitive system is a suspended wire, mounted on the top of the perimeter fence on insulators, which uses capacitance to detect the proximity of an intruder's body. A similar system is used to monitor the entire length of the Hong Kong border fence.

Perimeter, and other, security systems can be backed up with closed-circuit television. Slow-scan television can be used to send video signals from remote and isolated sites via telephone lines to a central control station. A two-way telephone link can command the cameras to pan, tilt or zoom, and a permanent video record of events at the remote site can be obtained if an alarm is triggered.

One purpose of future treaties controlling conventional arms will be to reduce the risk of surprise attack. The rapid analysis and communication of data will, therefore, be a crucial element of the verification of such treaties.

21

CONTROLLING THE ENVIRONMENTAL IMPACTS OF WAR

The Gulf War demonstrated yet again the horrific damage that can be done to the environment during modern warfare. The war brought home dramatically the need to evolve a new legal instrument to protect the environment in armed conflict. The purpose would be to outlaw the deliberate abuse of the environment as a weapon of war and the destruction of the environment by powerful modern weapons – including conventional ones.

Strategies to reduce the impact on the environment of military activities include: changing military postures to non-offensive defence; strengthening existing conventions relating to methods and means of warfare that cause damage to the environment by banning specific weapons that do unacceptable damage to the environment; negotiating a comprehensive and unambiguous environmental law of of war; controlling peacetime military activities that damage the environment; and negotiating a comprehensive nuclear test-ban treaty.

New powerful conventional weapons

Given the future likely patterns of violence, the potential environmental impact of very powerful conventional warheads, of improved yield-to-weight ratios, is considerable. An example of a new powerful conventional warhead is the fuel–air explosive, used by coalition forces during the Gulf War. The weapon produces an aerosol cloud of a substance like propylene oxide vapour. When mixed with air, the substance is very explosive, and the aerosol cloud, ignited when at its optimum size, produces a very powerful explosion, between five and ten times as effective, weight for weight, as high explosive.

Several clouds of fuel–air explosive can be formed close together so that when ignited they produce a huge explosion. This can be so large as to be equivalent to that of a low-yield nuclear explosion. People under the exploding cloud die from asphyxiation caused by physical damage to the membranes of their lungs. The fireball produced by the exploding aerosol cloud can kill and injure people on the edge of the explosion.

Cluster bombs and fragmentation munitions are other new conventional weapons. Exploding fragmentation bomblets can scatter small jagged chunks of metal over a large area. The fragments have razor-sharp edges, are very hot, and travel at high speeds. A rocket warhead can carry very large numbers of fragmentation munitions.

Most of the people in the range of the fragments are killed, many of them literally shredded. Those that escape immediate death often have multiple wounds, difficult to treat. Some fragmentation munitions are made of plastic. The fragments in the bodies of survivors do not then show up on X-rays, which greatly complicates medical treatment.

The Vought Multiple-Launch Rocket System (MLRS) fires rockets carrying cluster munitions with anti-personnel bomblets. Each rocket, about 4 metres long and 23 centimetres in diameter, contains 644 bomblets. A salvo of twelve rockets can be fired in about forty-five seconds, and there is a reload time of ten minutes. The range of MLRS is more than 30 kilometres. Each salvo of MLRS rockets, containing nearly 8,000 bomblets, can cover an area of about 60 acres with anti-personnel fragments, making it as lethal as a low-yield nuclear weapon.

Existing international conventions relating to the environment

Existing relevant international conventions are not adequate to outlaw the destruction of the environment by powerful modern weapons. These existing conventions include: the 1925 Geneva Protocol, prohibiting the use of bacteriological methods of warfare; the 1977 Protocol I on the Protection of Victims of International Armed Conflicts, additional to the 1949 Geneva Convention Relating to Protection of Victims of Armed Conflicts, prohibiting the use of methods and means of warfare that are intended or may be expected to cause widespread, long-term and severe damage to the natural environment; the 1977 Environmental Modification Convention, prohibiting the hostile use of environmental modification techniques which cause widespread, long-term or severe damage to the environment; and the 1980 Inhumane Weapon Convention, restricting the use of a few specific weapons, such as remotely delivered mines and incendiary weapons.

This list looks impressive, but the conventions are ambiguous and unclear, and neither comprehensive nor authoritative enough, in themselves, to constrain significantly military activities in armed conflict. The relevant articles in the 1977 Protocol, for example, are so general as to be susceptible to self-interpretation; they can be interpreted to mean what one wants them to mean, with the result that they are often interpreted to suit the interests of the interpreter. It is virtually impossible to judge which activities resulting in environmental damage in warfare are violations of existing international instruments.

Time for a new convention

The aftermath of the Gulf War, with its horrendous environmental destruction, may be the right legislative moment to mobilize political and public opinion in favour of the adoption of a comprehensive and unambiguous environmental law of war, including realistic means of enforcement, with perhaps an international tribunal to judge violations.

A recent conference in London, organized by Greenpeace, discussed the tenets on which a new convention to protect the environment in war should be based and proposed the following (Arkin *et al.* 1991):

Military interests should not be permitted to overrule environmental protection.

The environment needs to be protected in all armed conflict, not just in war.

No armed conflict should be permitted to damage the environment of a third party.

Military action should be ruled out if the environmental consequences are unknown or expected to lead to severe damage.

Each party should be held responsible for the environmental damage it has caused during armed conflict.

The use of weapons of mass destruction must be banned.

The environment should not be used as a weapon, and weapons aimed at the environment must be banned.

The indirect effects of warfare on the environment should be covered by the treaty.

The destruction of or damage to installations that can release dangerous radioactive or poisonous substances should be forbidden.

Nature parks and areas of special ecological importance should be classified as demilitarized zones.

The most effective way forward, in the first instance, may, however, be to prohibit the use of specific weapons that do unacceptable damage to the environment. This could most simply be done by strengthening existing conventions.

The decade of the 1990s is the United Nations decade of international law, intended to promote the supremacy of international law in the conduct of international relations. The evolution of an environmental law of war would be a most appropriate exercise during the decade.

22

THE PEACE DIVIDEND

Reductions in military spending after the Cold War

The extent of the reduction in world military expenditures, made possible by the end of the Cold War, will depend mainly on what happens to the military budgets of the USA and the former Soviet Union. In 1990, for example, these two countries together accounted for more than 60 per cent of the world total. A 5 per cent decrease in America's military budget and a roughly 10 per cent reduction in the Soviet one, were the main contributions to a decline in world military spending in 1990 of about 5 per cent. It is reasonable to expect similar annual declines for the next few years.

If this actually happens, it will amount to annual reductions in military expenditures of about $50,000 million, about the same amount that is currently given by governments to Third World countries in development aid. The developed countries, of course, will probably use most of any money saved from military budgets for domestic purposes, such as improving their own health and education services. But if the money were given to underdeveloped countries and allocated, for example, to health care it would be enough to double governmental health expenditures, providing enough resources to immunize every baby and to provide safe water and adequate sanitation to every village within ten years.

During the 1980s, the former Soviet Union probably spent about 20 per cent of its Gross Domestic Produce (GDP) on the military. The fifteen republics of the Commonwealth of Independent States have such enormous economic problems that they simply cannot afford to spend this much on the military. In January 1992, General James Clapper, the director of the US Defense Intelligence Agency reported that 'Over the last few years, [Soviet] defense spending has declined by approximately one quarter in real terms . . . . In Russia's recently announced defense proposal for the first quarter of this year, procurement appears to have been cut by about 80 per cent.'

171

Russia plans to spend no more than 5 per cent of GDP on the military, although its stated ambition to maintain a 1.5-million-strong army may push military spending closer to 10 per cent of GDP. The only other republics likely to retain significant military forces are the Ukraine and Khazakhstan.

The Americans plan much less dramatic cuts in their military budget. The Bush administration wants to spend $291,000 million on the military in fiscal year 1993, a 4.6 per cent decrease from the 1992 budget. By fiscal year 1997, under the administration's plan, the military budget would be 35 per cent lower in real terms than it was in the peak year of 1985, but it would still be higher *in real terms* than it was in 1980. The USA's military budget will probably remain above 5 per cent of GDP for the foreseeable future.

Most western European countries plan to reduce their military budgets. That of the UK, for example, will go down from 4 per cent of GDP in 1990 to about 3.5 per cent in 1995. Sweden, on the other hand, plans to increase its military spending by about 7 per cent in real terms.

Now that Soviet and American competition for client states in the Third World has largely ended we can expect that many Third World countries will feel increasingly secure as superpower intervention disappears; pressures to spend large sums on the military will correspondingly decrease. But there will be exceptions.

Today's biggest military spenders are in the Middle East: Iraq, Israel, Jordan, Oman, Saudi Arabia, Syria, and Yemen all typically spend more than 10 per cent of GDP on the military. Military budgets in the region after the Gulf War are unlikely to be reduced for the foreseeable future. We can also expect that military expenditures in countries in insecure regions – particularly North Korea, South Korea and Cuba – will remain high until they feel less threatened.

It is, therefore, not possible to make any general rule about the peace dividend following the end of the Cold War. The military budgets of the republics in the Commonwealth of Independent States are likely to be reduced significantly. And so may those of the eastern European countries. But those of most of the other European countries and of the USA are likely to be reduced by only a few per cent a year.

In the developing world, some countries will spend less on the military as tensions decrease and authoritarian governments democratize. But in regions where tensions remain high, such as the Middle East, military budgets are likely to continue to increase.

Trends in the global arms trade

The total value of the arms trade has been decreasing for the past few years. According to SIPRI, this value in 1991 was 25 per cent less than in 1990. This downward trend may well continue for the next few years. With arms producers desperate to secure new orders for weapons and the arms market contracting, competition for orders will become increasingly fierce. The large American defence corporations are the most likely to win.

In 1991, according to SIPRI, the USA accounted for 51 per cent of the global trade in major weapons (compared to 30 per cent in 1987); the Commonwealth of Independent States accounted for 18 per cent of the global arms trade (compared with the Soviet share of 39 per cent in 1987); European Community members accounted for about 20 per cent (compared to about 15 per cent in 1987), with Germany's share increasing while the shares of France and the UK decreased.

The Middle East has been replaced by Asia as the main market for major weapons. The Middle East accounted for 32 per cent of arms imports in 1982; it accounted for 21 per cent in 1991. Asia accounted for 15 per cent of arms imports in 1982 and 34 per cent in 1991.

The industrialized countries rather than Third World countries are increasingly important arms importers. The share of the rich countries in the global arms trade has increased from about 33 per cent to 1987 to over 50 per cent today. Increased imports by Japan and – despite the end of the Cold War – the NATO countries mainly account for this trend.

A very important new factor affecting the dynamics of the arms trade is the disintegration of the Soviet Union, the largest exporter of arms for most of the 1980s. In 1990, the value of Soviet arms exports sharply decreased. Compared to earlier years it roughly halved and, for the first time for nearly a decade, the USSR took second place to the USA in the rank order of arms exporters.

Economic consequences of the peace dividend

An important aspect of reductions in military budgets is the effect on employment, including the redundancy of military personnel, reductions in the numbers of civilians directly employed out of the military budget, and the indirect effects on workers in defence industries of changes in the procurement of weapons. It is the fear of creating unemployment, and in some cases of increasing already high unemployment, which prevents many governments from making deep cuts in military budgets.

There is a very wide range of numbers of jobs supported by military budgets. Studies in Canada, France, West Germany, Norway, Sweden, the UK and the USA have shown that the number of jobs per $1,000 million of military expenditure varies from 23.3 for Sweden to 63.1 for France, with an average of 46.2. On average, military expenditure supported about 4 per cent of the labour force in these countries, but the studies showed significant regional and industrial variations. Military expenditure in these countries also averaged about 4 per cent of GDP.

In the UK, for example, military spending on defence equipment in 1987 supported the direct employment of 310,000 and the indirect employment of 255,000, for a total of 565,000 people (4.3 per cent of the total labour force). The impact of British military spending is concentrated on a relatively small number of industries. According to official figures for 1985, commodities purchased by government defence spending accounted for: 59.7 per cent of total demand for the ship-building industry; 32.4 per cent of total demand for the aerospace-equipment industry; 14.9 per cent of total demand for the electronics industry; and 3.2 per cent of total demand for the construction industry. In other industries it accounted for less than 3 per cent.

Using a multisectoral macro-economic model to evaluate the impact of reducing UK defence spending to half of its 1992 value by the year 2000, Barker *et al.* concluded that such a reduction, without appropriate planning, 'would reduce GDP 3.5 per cent and increase unemployment by 0.46 million. If the released expenditures are allocated to other government current and capital expenditures, however, the net effect would be to decrease unemployment by 0.52 million and increase output above base by 1.84 per cent between 1992 and 2000.'

There would be 'potential problems at industry, company, region, and local community levels which will need to be dealt with'. But these problems at the regional or local-community level should 'be no worse than those experienced over the last decade and with careful planning could be made painless' (Barker *et al.*, November 1991).

Similar studies in other countries draw the same conclusions. If sensibly done, cutting military budgets can significantly improve a country's economic performance. But it must be emphasized that, globally and domestically, by far the most beneficial peace dividend would come from reductions in the resources given to military science.

The global consequences of devoting large resources, particularly scientific manpower, to military R & D has already been discussed. There are also adverse consequences for domestic economies. If these resources were used to improve technological innovation in the civilian sector, labour productivity and economic growth would benefit. The poor economic performance of countries like the former Soviet Union, the USA and the UK, compared with countries like Japan and Germany, is largely due to the considerably larger resources devoted by the former countries to military R & D.

The dismantlement of nuclear weapons

Another feature of the peace dividend is the need to dismantle nuclear weapons removed from the nuclear arsenals because of nuclear disarmament measures which are a sequel to the end of the Cold War. The 1991 Strategic Arms Reduction Treaty (START) and Soviet–American announcements of unilateral reductions in numbers of tactical nuclear weapons will, if carried out, cut the total number of nuclear weapons operationally deployed by the United States and the former Soviet Union from about 45,000 to about 7,000. Thousands of nuclear weapons will be dismantled because of these obligations and because of the retirement of aged and obsolete weapons.

Dismantlement involves: removing the nuclear weapons or nuclear delivery systems from their deployed positions and transporting them to central storage areas; where necessary, removing the warhead from its delivery system (such as a missile); cutting open and removing the outer casing; removing the container of tritium, if the explosive power of the warhead is 'boosted' by fusion material; if the weapon is thermonuclear, removing the lithium deuteride and the highly enriched uranium (HEU) from the secondary (fusion) stage and then removing the high explosives surrounding the plutonium, or HEU, or both in the primary (fission) stage (this fissile material is called the 'pit'); or, if the weapon is just a nuclear-fission weapon, removing the high explosives surrounding the pit; removing the beryllium reflector and the uranium tamper surrounding the pit; and removing the fissile material in the pit.

Non-nuclear components can be destroyed; for example, the conventional high explosive can be burned and electronic components discarded. Normally, the nuclear components will be melted down to change their form to keep secret details of the pit – the original machined size and shape of the plutonium and/or HEU pieces, the amounts of non-nuclear metals alloyed with the fissile material in the pit, the amounts of fissile material used, and the isotopic composition of the fissile material.

Because of the presence of radioactive decay products, such as isotopes of americium, non-nuclear alloy material, and non-nuclear material used to coat (and make airtight) the fissile material, the pits will be chemically reprocessed to separate out and purify the plutonium and HEU. These fissile materials will then either be stored, in metallic or oxide form, or permanently disposed of.

Nuclear weapons must be dismantled with great care. Each ex-Soviet weapon is, like most American ones, probably a sealed unit, filled with innert gas. The gas will probably be radioactive, and its release would be a hazard to workers. Also, some of the non-nuclear material in the weapons, such as beryllium, is highly toxic.

The conventional high explosive in the warhead must, of course, be handled with care. Many ex-Soviet, and some American, weapons do not have insensitive high explosives (less prone to shock than ordinary explosives). Also, safety devices in typical ex-Soviet weapons are much less sophisticated than those in their American counterparts. Some of the older ex-Soviet weapons probably do not have safety devices.

The dismantling of nuclear weapons will involve the removal of large amounts of fissile material. American nuclear weapons contain a total of about 100 tonnes of weapons-grade plutonium (plutonium containing more than 93 per cent of the isotope plutonium-239) and 500 tonnes of HEU (containing more than 90 per cent of the isotope uranium-235). Ex-Soviet nuclear weapons probably contain about 125 tonnes of weapons-grade plutonium and about 600 tonnes of highly enriched uranium.

The fissile materials removed from nuclear weapons could be stored in high-security stores. But permanent disposal of these materials may be required by future treaties to prevent their re-use in weapons, or it may be preferred to reduce both the risk that some fissile material may be stolen and the considerable expense of indefinite storage.

Several methods of disposal are being discussed. Plutonium and HEU could be used as fuel in civil reactors, thermal or breeder. HEU could be used to fuel naval reactors in warships and submarines. Plutonium and HEU could be mixed with high-level radioactive waste to make it difficult to re-use the materials in nuclear weapons without reprocessing,.

Other methods include deep-sea burial, firing the materials into the sun, and transmutation by changing the atomic number of atoms by bombardment by high-energy particles so that the new isotopes have shorter half-lives (the technology for large-scale transmutation does not yet exist).

Dismantling nuclear weapons is a lengthy process. If, for example, the ex-Soviet arsenal is to be reduced from the current 29,000 nuclear weapons to, say, 5,000, at a rate of about 1,200 a year (apparently the capacity of Russian dismantling facilities), the process will take about twenty years. In the meantime, the weapons will have to be stored. Keeping large numbers of stored nuclear weapons secure from theft and adequately maintained, to minimize the risk of accidental explosion, is a difficult and expensive business.

The Americans have offered Russia $400 million to help them build modern facilities to store nuclear weapons before dismantlement and to store fissile materials after dismantlement. This will not be enough. The British government should chip in some more.

REFERENCES

Albright, D. (1987), 'Civilian inventories of plutonium and highly enriched uranium', in Paul Leventhal and Yonah Alexander (eds), *Preventing Nuclear Terrorism*, Lexington, Mass.: Lexington Books.

Albright, D. and Feiveson, H. A. (1991), 'Plutonium recycling and the problem of nuclear proliferation', in Frank Barnaby (ed.), *Plutonium and Security: The Military Aspects of the Plutonium Economy*, London: Macmillan Press.

Anthony, I. and Wulf, H. (1990), 'The trade in major conventional weapons', *World Armaments and Disarmament*, SIPRI Yearbook 1990, Oxford: Oxford University Press.

Anthony, I., Allebeck, A. C., Hagemeyer-Gaverus, G., Miggiano, P. and Wulf, W. (1991), 'The trade in major conventional weapons', *World Armaments and Disarmament*, SIPRI Yearbook 1991, Oxford: Oxford University Press.

Arkin, W. M., Durrant, D. and Cherni, M. (May 1991), *On Impact. Modern Warfare and the Environment: A Case Study of the Gulf War*, London: Greenpeace.

Arms Control Association (October 1991), 'Impact of the Bush nuclear weapons initiative', *Arms Control Today* 21, 8.

Barker, T., Dunne, P. and Smith, R. (November 1991), 'Measuring the peace dividend in the United Kingdom', *Journal of Peace Research* 28, 1.

Barnaby, Frank (ed.) (1989), *Handbook of Verification Technologies*, London: Macmillan Press.

Barnaby, Frank (ed.) (1991), *Plutonium and Security: The Military Aspects of the Plutonium Economy*, London: Macmillan Press.

Beker, A. (1986), 'A regional non-proliferation treaty for the Middle East', in L. R. Beres (ed.), *Security or Armageddon: Israel's Nuclear Strategy*, Lexington, Mass.: Lexington Books.

Beres, L. R. (ed.) (1986), *Security of Armageddon: Israel's Nuclear Strategy*, Lexington, Mass.: Lexington Books.

Boserup, A., Robinson, J. P., Nield, R. and Hirdman, S. (1971), *The Prevention of CBW*, Stockholm: Almqvist & Wiksell.

British American Security Information Council (BASIC) (November 1991), *European Nuclear Weapons – Modernization and Expansion*, London: BASIC.

Brzoska, M. and Ohlson, T. (1986), *Arms Production in the Third World*, London: Taylor & Francis.

Calvocoressi, P. (1987), *A Time for Peace*, London: Hutchinson.

Colby, W. (1979), in *Military Implications of the Treaty on the Limitation of Strategic Offensive Arms and Protocol Thereto (Salt II Treaty)*, Hearings before the Committee on Armed Services (SASC Hearings), US Senate, 96th Congress, First

Session, Washington, DC: US Government Printing Office, Part 3, 9, 10, 11 and 16 October, p. 1015.

Congressional Research Service (1991), *Conventional Arms Transfers to the Third World, 1983–90*, Report to Congress, 2 August, Washington, DC: Library of Congress.

Dean, J. (1989), 'Verifying NATO–Warsaw Pact force reductions and stabilizing measures', in Frank Barnaby (ed.), *Handbook of Verification Technologies*, London: Macmillan Press.

Donnelly, W. H. (1991), 'US policy for plutonium: civilian use, non-proliferation and nuclear arms reduction', in Frank Barnaby (ed.), *Plutonium and Security: The Military Aspects of the Plutonium Economy*, London: Macmillan Press.

Ferm, R. (1991), 'Nuclear explosions', *World Armaments and Disarmament*, SIPRI Yearbook 1991, Oxford: Oxford University Press.

Goldblat, J. and Bernauer, T. (1991), *The Third Review of the Biological Weapons Convention: Issues and Proposals*, United Nations Institute for Disarmament Research, United Nations publication no. GV.E.91.0.5, New York: United Nations.

Hansen, C. (1988), *US Nuclear Weapons: The Secret History*, New York: Orion Books.

Harris, R. and Paxman, J. (1982), *A Higher Form of Killing: The Secret Story of Gas and Germ Warfare*, London: Chatto & Windus.

International Atomic Energy Agency (1991), 'Nuclear power status around the world', *IAEA Bulletin 33*, 3.

International Chernobyl Project (1991), *The Radiological Consequences in the USSR of the Chernobyl Accident: Assessment of Health and Environment Effects and Evaluation of Protective Measures*, Vienna: International Atomic Energy Agency.

International Foundation for the Survival and Development of Humanity (1991), *Toward a Comprehensive Nuclear-Warhead Test Ban*, Moscow: IFSDH.

International Institute for Strategic Studies (1991), *The Military Balance, 1991–1992*, London: IISS.

International Physicians for the Prevention of Nuclear War (1991), *Radioactive Heaven and Earth*, London: Zed Books.

Jasani, B. and Barnaby, F. (1984), *Verification Technologies*, London: Berg Publishers/Centre for International Peacebuilding.

Karp, A. (June 1988), 'The frantic Third World quest for ballistic missiles', *Bulletin of the Atomic Scientists* 44, 5.

Karp, A. (1991), 'Ballistic missile proliferation', *World Armaments and Disarmament*, SIPRI Yearbook 1991, Oxford: Oxford University Press.

Kellen, K. (1987), 'The potential for nuclear terrorism: a discussion', in Paul Leventhal and Yonah Alexander (eds), *Preventing Nuclear Terrorism*, Lexington, Mass.: Lexington Books.

Krass, A. S. (1985), *Verification: How Much Is Enough?*, London: Taylor & Francis.

Leventhal, Paul and Alexander, Yonah (eds) (1987), *Preventing Nuclear Terrorism*, Lexington, Mass.: Lexington Books.

Lovins, A. B. (1980), 'Nuclear weapons and power-reactor plutonium', *Nature*, 28 February, and typographical corrections 13 March.

Lundin, S. J. (1989), 'Chemical and biological warfare: developments in 1988', *World Armaments and Disarmament*, SIPRI Yearbook 1989, Oxford: Oxford University Press.

179

Lundin, S. J. (1990), 'Chemical and biological warfare: developments in 1989', *World Armaments and Disarmament*, SIPRI Yearbook 1990, Oxford: Oxford University Press.

Lundin, S. J. and Stock, T. (1991), 'Chemical and biological warfare: developments in 1990', *World Armaments and Disarmament*, SIPRI Yearbook 1991, Oxford: Oxford University Press.

Lundin, S. J., Robinson, J. P. P. and Trapp, R. (1988), 'Chemical and biological warfare: developments in 1987', *World Armaments and Disarmament*, SIPRI Yearbook 1988, Oxford: Oxford University Press.

Lyddon, P. and Lingwood, M. (June 1988), 'Verification for conventional arms control', *Bulletin of the Council for Arms Control* 38.

Mark, J. Carson, Taylor, T., Eyster, E., Maraman, W. and Wechsler, J. (1987), 'Can terrorists build nuclear weapons?', in Paul Leventhal and Yonah Alexander (eds), *Preventing Nuclear Terrorism*, Lexington, Mass.: Lexington Books.

Nelson, D. N. (Spring 1991), 'Europe's unstable east', *Foreign Policy* 82.

Norris, R. S., Fieldhouse, R. W., Cochran, T. B. and Arkin, W. M. (1991), 'Nuclear weapons', *World Armaments and Disarmament*, SIPRI Yearbook 1991, Oxford: Oxford University Press.

Novick, R. and Shulman, S. (1990), 'New forms of biological warfare', in S. Wright (ed.), *Preventing a Biological Arms Race*, Cambridge, Mass.: MIT Press.

Nuclear Proliferation and Safeguards (1977), US Congress, Office of Technology Assessment, Washington, DC: OTA.

Reconnaissance Handy Book (1980), Long Beach, Calif.: McDonnell Douglas Corporation, p. 125.

Robinson, J. P. (1971), *The Rise of CB Weapons*, Stockholm: Almqvist & Wiksell.

Robinson, J. P., Heden, C.-G. and Schreeb, H. von (1973), *CB Weapons Today*, Stockholm: Almqvist & Wiksell.

Rose, S. (1987), 'Biotechnology at war', *New Scientist*, 19 March.

Rosenberg, B. H. and Burck, G. (1990), 'Verification of compliance with the Biological Weapons Convention', in S. Wright (ed.), *Preventing a Biological Arms Race*, Cambridge, Mass.: MIT Press.

Rotblat, J. (1981), *Nuclear Radiation in Warfare*, London: Taylor & Francis.

Sigmund, W. and Sigmund, E. (October 1991), 'UNSCOM reports on Iraqi CBW capability', *CBW News* 5.

Simpson, J. (October 1991), 'NPT stronger after Iraq', *Bulletin of the Atomic Scientists* 47, 8.

Spector, Leonard (1987), *Going Nuclear*, Cambridge, Mass.: Ballinger.

Stockholm International Peace Research Institute (SIPRI) (1991), *World Armaments and Disarmament*, SIPRI Yearbook 1991, Oxford: Oxford University Press.

United Nations (1991), *Report on the Fourth IAEA On-Site Inspection in Iraq under Security Council Resolution 687 (1991)*, New York: United Nations.

United States Arms Control and Disarmament Agency (1991), *A START Briefing Book*, Washington, DC: State Department, 29 July.

Westing, A. H. (1976), *Ecological Consequences of the Second Indochina War*, Stockholm: Almqvist & Wiksell.

Willrich, M. and Taylor, T. (1974), *Nuclear Theft and Safeguards*, Cambridge, Mass.: Ballinger.

World Commerce in Nuclear Materials (November 1987), Washington, DC: US Department of Defense.

Wright, S. (ed.) (1990), *Preventing a Biological Arms Race*, Cambridge, Mass.: MIT Press.

REFERENCES

Wulf, H. (1991), 'Arms production', *World Armaments and Disarmament*, SIPRI Yearbook 1991, Oxford: Oxford University Press.

Wulf, H. and Anthony, I. (1991), 'The proliferation of conventional weapons and prospects for control', paper presented to SIPRI Conference, Saltsjobaden, 12–14 November.

INDEX